DocDE

LARRY DIXON

DOCDEVOS

Ten-Minute Daily Devotionals
on the Great Doctrines
of the Christian Faith

✠ CHRISTIAN PUBLICATIONS, INC.
CAMP HILL, PENNSYLVANIA

✠CHRISTIAN PUBLICATIONS, INC.
3825 Hartzdale Drive, Camp Hill, PA 17011
www.christianpublications.com

Faithful, biblical publishing since 1883

DocDEVOs
ISBN: 0-87509-890-8
LOC Control Number: 2001-134119
© 2002 by Larry Dixon
All rights reserved
Printed in the United States of America

02   03   04   05   06   5   4   3   2   1

Dedication

To my wife Linda, who has modeled a daily
walk with the Lord and who challenges me
to do the same. Thank you for over thirty years
of encouragement in the truths
of the Christian faith.

Contents

Introduction

Section Three: Great Is the God We Adore

Introduction

Have you ever felt like a spiritual ninety-eight-pound weakling when it comes to defending your Christian faith? You're tired of the "isms" of the world kicking sand in your face, and you want to *do something* about it!

When your local neighborhood Jehovah's Witnesses or Mormons ring your doorbell, do you find yourself engaged in the time-honored Christian game of "hide 'n seek"? When your pastor asks the congregation on Sunday morning to turn to "Second Concordances," are you the only one *not* laughing while you're flipping pages as quickly as you can? When the Gallup Poll people call your home to ask what the "typical American Christian believes," do they hang up before you've even answered their first question?

Then this devotional book is for you! The purpose of *DOC DEVOs* is to introduce you to the basic beliefs of the Christian faith in an easy-to-read, daily format. Each daily reading examines the central truth of a particular doctrine (referred to as "The Knowledge Nugget"), applies it to daily experience (in a section called "Real Life Says . . ."), then suggests how you might pray about it (the part I call "But, Lord . . ."). Finally, a thought-provoking saying or summary statement (entitled "To Ponder . . .") concludes the day's reading.

DOC DEVOs steers clear of religious jargon and technical language. However, at the back of the book is a glossary of theological terms with basic definitions. Both the new believer in Jesus Christ as well as the older Christian who wants to grow steadily in his or her understanding of the fundamentals of the faith will benefit from the daily discipline of *DOC DEVOs*. Each day's entry will build on the previous day's reading, so keeping up with the series is important.

The devotionals in *DOC DEVOs* will focus on the *fundamentals*, not the *distinctives*, of the Christian faith. By the term "fundamentals" we mean those truths which are clearly taught in Scripture (the deity of Christ, the goodness of God, the truthfulness of the Bible, for example) and on which all genuine Christians must agree. The term "distinctives" refers to those particular perspectives or beliefs which are less clear in the Bible, and about which Christians are free to agree or disagree with one another in love.

One of the difficulties in evangelical Christianity these days is that one man's "essential" is another man's "distinctive"! For example, many Christians believe that Christ will not return for His Church until *after* the Tribulation. Others believe that He will "catch away" ("rapture") His Bride (the Church) *prior* to His second coming. When I discuss such beliefs, I attempt to look at the issues from several viewpoints, without seeking to "convert" the reader to my personal view. As one preacher put it, "The main thing is to keep the main thing the main thing." The purpose of *DOC DEVOs* is to concentrate on the "one faith" which all Christians should know and enjoy.

This volume contains three sections. "First Things First" deals with a number of issues which need to be discussed *before* one dives into the character of God, the nature of salvation or other specific areas of doctrine. We will tackle such questions as:

- What is meant by "faith"?
- How is the term "theology" to be understood?
- What about the issue of *tolerance*?
- What is the connection between what one *believes* and how one *behaves*?
- Should we be glad that the Bible is not a systematic theology textbook?

The second section, entitled "The Absolute Need for an Absolute Authority," will ask such questions as:

- What are the *sources* from which many people get their beliefs?
- What is the role of the Bible in determining what we believe—and what we *don't*?
- Are we to trust our own experiences, reason or intuition when it comes to the Christian faith?
- What if I just don't like reading the Bible?
- How do we know that our Bibles are complete?
- Are there other holy books that should be consulted for our doctrine?
- What is involved in being a "Berean believer"?
- Isn't everyone entitled to his or her own interpretation of the Bible?
- What are some of the important characteristics of the Bible as the Word of God?
- What about those who claim to hear God's voice?

The third section is entitled "Great Is the God We Adore." These thirty devotionals will focus on the character and works of our Creator. Some of the questions we will discuss are:

- Is there anything that God *cannot* do?
- What do we mean when we say we Christians are *monotheists*?
- What about the doctrine of the Trinity?
- Does God ever "hide" Himself?
- What does the Bible teach about God's mercy, justice, faithfulness, goodness and *jealousy*?

These and many other issues will be our diet for the next three months. So, set a specific time to curl up with this book, have your Bible close by and get ready to grow like a weed. And may the God of truth encourage your heart so that, as one preacher puts it, you will "grow in grace and not groan in disgrace!"

Section One:

First Things First

A Brief Preview

"It doesn't matter what you believe, as long as you are sincere!" say many in our society.

Really?

The first section of this volume covers such issues as the meaning of faith, what doctrine is and why we should study it and why tolerance should not be confused with truth. Because every Christian ought to be a student of the truths of God, we will discuss the value of heresy, the help which philosophy can provide us and the benefit and dangers of creeds.

Growing in our knowledge of doctrine is not merely mental, however. We will also look at how what we believe has to be shown by how we behave, both inside the church (right practices) and in the world (godly conduct). We must become personally committed to doctrinal growth so that we can identify untruth in its many disguises and help other Christians who are wandering from the faith.

Doctrine has gotten a lot of "bad press" in many circles, so we will also discuss the difference between Christian belief and superstition and why studying biblical doctrine need not be a boring task.

Everybody Lives by Faith!

The term "faith" may refer to one's confidence in God or, as we'll see today, to the content of truth God has given by His grace.

Faith does not deny facts. It does not turn away from reality. But faith understands that beyond the realities of this world there is a greater Reality.

(John H. Stevens)

Faith is believing in things when common sense tells you not to.

(*Miracle on 34th Street*)

Dear friends, although I was very eager to write to you about the salvation we share, I felt I had to write and urge you to contend for the faith that was once for all entrusted to the saints.

(Jude 3)

The Knowledge Nugget

The term "faith" may be used to refer to one's trust in God and His Word (Hebrews 11:1). We encourage people to "have faith" or talk about someone "acting in faith." Our confidence in life is not to be in ourselves or the things of this world, but in our Creator and Redeemer and in His communication to us through His Word, the Bible.

The term "faith" may also be used to refer to that specific content of truth which He has given to us (the Christian "faith"). In our verse for today, Jude, the half brother of Jesus, encourages his readers to "contend for the faith that was once for all entrusted to the saints" (Jude 3). In our study of the faith, that is, of the doctrines of biblical Christianity, we are to affirm what God has told us in the Bible, then seek to present—and defend—those truths before the world.

Real Life Says . . .

But "real life" suggests that no one finally has the truth, certainly not in eternal matters. Each person must create his or her own spiritual reality, says our world, and no person has the right to claim that only his (or her) faith is ultimately true. Others suggest that having any kind of faith is for the weak. The strong of this world don't need any religious orientation to live successful lives—or so they think.

A newspaper once had a column entitled "The Answer Man." Readers could send in any question they wanted answered. One question that was sent in read, "How does an elevator work?" "The Answer Man" responded, "An elevator is essentially a small room dangling over a very deep shaft, held up by thin cables that are maintained by building employees who have tremendous trouble just keeping all the toilets working."

This shows that everyone, in some sense, lives by what we might call faith. No one has the FBI do a background check on the young man who serves them a burger and fries at a fast-food restaurant. We ask total strangers for directions (although men struggle with the concept!) and trust them not to lead us over a cliff. And we never do a safety inspection on an elevator before we use it—we just step in.

Christian faith, however, is *not* gullibility, wishful thinking, mass hypnosis or auto-suggestion. Faith, as presented in the Bible, is only as good as the object in which it is placed.

In Jude's battle plan for believers, his challenge to us to "contend for the *faith*" does not refer to our confidence in God, but to the specific doctrines which should guide followers of Christ. This content of truth, this "faith" that we are to fight for, is described in a unique way. Jude calls it the "once-for-all-entrusted-to-the-saints" faith, which means that God will never edit His truth, abridge the Word of God or change its content.

But before we can defend it, we must know it. And that's what these devotionals are all about.

But Lord . . .

Lord, I don't know all that I should believe. Expand my understanding of, and my obedience to, the truths which You have revealed for my good and Your glory. Help me to live today looking for ways to humbly stand for Your truth. In Jesus' name, Amen.

To Ponder . . .

"People are driven from the Church not so much by stern truth that makes them uneasy as by weak nothings that make them contemptuous." (George Buttrick)

A Faith That Forms

If "faith" refers to the content of truth which God has given us, then Christian growth comes as we learn—and put into practice—what His Word teaches.

Faith is not something one "loses"; we merely cease to shape our lives by it.

(George Bernanos)

The atheistic German philosopher, Friedrich Nietzsche, made the following surly remark to some Christians one day: "If you want me to believe in your Redeemer, then you've got to look a lot more redeemed."

Do not conform any longer to the pattern of this world, but be transformed by the renewing of your mind.

(Romans 12:2)

The Knowledge Nugget

A pastor ran into a former church member on the street one day.

"How are things going, Tom?" the pastor asked.

"Well, Reverend, things couldn't be worse! I lost my job last week, the bank is repossessing my car, and my mother-in-law just moved into our basement. It's enough to make a man lose his religion!"

"Sorry to hear of your troubles, Tom," said the pastor. "But it seems to me that it's enough to make a man *use* his religion!"

It's commonly said that "what you don't know can't hurt you"—but is that really true? If we don't know that God is everywhere, the resulting loneliness could cripple our Christian lives. If we know little about the doctrine of God's goodness, then we may struggle for years, afraid to surrender ourselves completely to Him. The doctrines of the Christian faith should not only inform us of what we need to know, but should also *form* us into the people we should be.

Ignorance of the truths of biblical Christianity hinders growth in godliness. While it is quite possible to know the facts of the Christian faith but remain unchanged, the normal Christian life is one in which God uses His truth to transform us. What we believe should affect how we behave.

Real Life Says . . .

"Churches are full of hypocrites!" How many times have you heard someone say that? I know one pastor who responds, "I know exactly what you mean. But our church is big enough for one more! Why don't you come join us?" That may not be the best way to attract seekers to Christ, but it illustrates the fact that all of us probably believe far more than we behave.

My parents came to know Christ through the ministry of evangelist Leighton Ford. He once stated, "God loves you enough to accept you the way you are, but He loves you too much to leave you that way." The first half of his statement illustrates salvation: We do not clean up our lives to get saved; God takes us as we are. But the second half of Ford's statement is talking about growth in the Christian life. God loves us too much to allow us to stay where we are spiritually.

But how does He shape and remold us into the image of Christ? Romans 12:2 tells us, "be transformed by the renewing of your mind." The mind is renewed by *truth*—and the Word of God, the Bible, is the truth we need if we want to be renewed. Whether we really believe the truths of God's Word will be revealed by the Christlike changes that take place in our lives.

The story is told of a band of explorers in Africa who hired some villagers to help them in their journey through the jungle. The group set out and pushed on without stopping for several days. Finally the tribesmen sat down, refusing to go any further. When asked why they were stopping, the eldest among them said, "We've been going too fast. We must pause and wait for our souls to catch up with our bodies." Perhaps we need to pause and wait for our behavior to catch up to our belief.

But Lord . . .

Lord, forgive my arrogance in thinking that I know all I need to know, believe all I need to believe and practice all I ought to practice. In Jesus' name, Amen.

To Ponder . . .

We cannot become what we need to be by remaining what we are. (Max De Pree)

Who Needs Theology?

Theology: The study of the truths of God as set forth in the Bible. The word literally means the study of God and the things of God.

Theology: the effort to explain the unknowable in terms no one understands.

(Anonymous)

If you believe what you like in the gospel and reject what you don't like, it is not the gospel you believe, but yourself.

(Augustine)

Therefore let us leave the elementary teachings about Christ and go on to maturity, not laying again the foundation of repentance from acts that lead to death, and of faith in God, instruction about baptisms, the laying on of hands, the resurrection of the dead, and eternal judgment. And God permitting, we will do so.

(Hebrews 6:1-3)

The Knowledge Nugget

As the guest preacher in a small church, I walked up to the pulpit to begin speaking and found a note taped to the lecturn, right where my sermon notes were to be put. It read, "Please don't give us

THEOLOGY! Just give us JESUS!" I was sorely tempted to tell them that to give them Jesus meant I had to give them good theology, but I behaved myself.

The term "theology" is made up of two words: *theos*, which means "God" or the "things of God," and *logos*, which means "study of" or "words of." Theology, in its simplest definition, is the study of God and the things of God.

A man was asked by an interviewer, "Sir, what do you believe?"

"I believe what my church believes," he replied.

"Well," asked the reporter, "what does your church believe?"

"The church believes what I believe!"

"That's interesting," the reporter said. "Well, what do you and your church believe?"

The man thought for a moment and then replied, "We believe the same thing, dummy!"

In the first two devotionals, we saw that the Christian faith is a specific content of truth given by God for our good—and for our growth. Although the term "theology" is found nowhere in the Bible (the term "Trinity" isn't either, for that matter), the Bible presents teachings (doctrines) which ought to be understood, embraced and defended by believers in Jesus Christ.

Real Life Says . . .

Our culture often confuses opinion and truth, so it is essential for a Christian to know the doctrines—the theology—of the Word of God. The truths of the Bible remind us that real life is defined by the real Life-Giver. Learning His truth prepares us to live in this world of unreality!

The Bible is not a systematic theology textbook (a point we will look at in Section Two), but the theology presented in its pages should lead a Christian to become like Christ. If we want to mature in the life of faith, we need to learn Christianity's doctrines.

When the writer of Hebrews says (in the passage quoted earlier) that we are to "leave the elementary teachings" of the Christian faith, he does not mean that we are to *abandon* them. He lists several doctrines as "elementary teachings," such as repentance, faith, the resurrection of the dead and eternal judgment. The writer to the Hebrews is challenging us to grow deeper in doctrine. In fact, he uses two pictures in the preceding chapter for driving home that point:

1. In 5:11-12, he uses the image of a classroom to rebuke the Hebrews for taking so long to grow from students into spiritual teachers. He even says they need "remedial education" in the fundamentals of the faith!
2. In 5:13-14, he compares spiritual growth to food. The one who is a spiritual infant is still living on theological milk. He or she needs to move on to the solid meat of God's Word.

Who needs theology? The biblical answer is, *we all do!*

But Lord . . .

Lord, I am sure I don't know or believe everything I should, and I may even believe some things that I shouldn't—things that are contrary to Your Word. Help me to grow in Your truth today, so that I will know what I believe—and why. In Jesus' name, Amen.

To Ponder . . .

To love God with my mind means I will embrace His truth and be stretched by His Spirit through His Word.

Who You Calling a "Theologian"?

A "theologian" is someone who studies the truths of God as revealed in the Bible, the Word of God. A professional theologian earns his living by teaching those truths.

A church that neither is interested in theology nor has the capacity to think theologically is a church that will be rapidly submerged beneath the waves of modernity. It is a church for whom Christian faith will rapidly lose its point . . . and a church whose interests are thus adrift is one that no longer is an audience for whom theologians can think. They are on the point of becoming artists whose work no one bothers to view.

(David Wells)

We dare not confine theology to seminary coffee shops where professors of students play mental badminton. It affects all of us.

(Philip Yancey)

"Let not the wise man boast of his wisdom
   or the strong man boast of his strength
   or the rich man boast of his riches,
but let him who boasts boast about this:
   that he understands and knows me,
that I am the LORD, who exercises kindness,
   justice and righteousness on earth,
   for in these I delight," declares the LORD.

(Jeremiah 9:23-24)

The Knowledge Nugget

It was said before that the term *theology* comes from the Greek words for "God" and "the study of." Some scholars suggest that the second part of the word might also mean "the praise of." The term *theology*, then, may mean either "the study of God," or "the praise of God and His truths." Taken in that sense, shouldn't *every* follower of Jesus Christ be a theologian?

I make a distinction between a *theologian* (lower case) and a *Theologian* (upper case). Every Christian should be a lower-case theologian; every believer ought to desire to know God and the things of God. An upper-case Theologian, on the other hand, is one who pursues formal education in Bible and theology and teaches courses in doctrine. We can't all be upper-case Theologians, but their "art" is crucially needed to keep the church from drifting aimlessly in the ocean of life, tossed to and fro by the next wave of unbiblical thought. We need to pray for and encourage those who study and teach God's truth, so *we* can think rightly!

Real Life Says . . .

Have you noticed how often anti-theology statements are made *in churches*? For example, one of my students told me his pastor once said, "The worst kind of Christian that you can be is a walking theologian!" Well, I believe that the Apostle Paul was a "walking theologian," that he lived what he taught and loved the One about whom he spoke. Perhaps the preacher meant that it is a sad case if one is *only* a "walking theologian" and not a practicing one. But I didn't ask him, because I might have been tempted to say something about *preachers*—even though I'm one too!

A professional Theologian (upper case) worth his salt will have a mind *and* heart longing to know God and the things of God. And we who recognize that we are all theologians (lower case) had better keep the main thing the main thing. As Jeremiah puts it,

"Let not the wise man boast of his wisdom
 or the strong man boast of his strength
 or the rich man boast of his riches,
but let him who boasts boast about this:
 that he understands and knows me,
that I am the LORD, who exercises kindness,
 justice and righteousness on earth,
 for in these I delight," declares the LORD.
(Jeremiah 9:23-24)

The believer in Jesus Christ is to consciously forsake any pride in his own wisdom, strength or riches (note the Apostle Paul in Philippians 3:4-11). But he is not to give up "boasting" completely! He is to delve deeply into the character of his God—and boast in the knowledge of the Lord. Aren't you glad you know the Lord? Then get excited—and brag about your Savior! And wear your "theologian" name tag proudly!

But Lord . . .

Lord, forgive me for belittling those who know the truths of Your Word. Please give me insight today into how I can be a better theologian, how I can love You more, and how I can boast about Your grace. In Jesus' name, Amen.

To Ponder . . .

Knowing theology without knowing God is nothing to brag about!

Don't You Just Hate Intolerance?

Tolerance may be defined as defending the right of others to believe what they want to believe. This is not the same as suggesting that all opinions are of equal validity.

Tolerance is the virtue of men who don't believe in anything.

(G.K. Chesterton)

The danger [students] have been taught to fear from absolutism is not error but intolerance.... Openness is the great insight of our times. The true believer is the real danger.... The point is not to correct the mistakes and really be right; rather it is not to think you are right at all.... The purpose of their education is not to make them scholars but to provide them with a moral virtue—openness.

(Allan Bloom)

Make every effort to keep the unity of the Spirit through the bond of peace. There is one body and one Spirit—just as you were called to one hope when you were called—one Lord, one faith, one baptism; one God and Father of all, who is over all and through all and in all.

(Ephesians 4:3-6)

The Knowledge Nugget

Because the Christian faith contains rational content and involves acceptance of certain truths, the study of that faith involves turning away from non-truth. Although we should respect those of other convictions, we must affirm what the Bible affirms and deny what the Bible denies. To be "tolerant" of another's viewpoint does not mean that we abandon the concept of truth. We must be faithful to the One who said, "I am the way and the *truth* and the life. No one comes to the Father except through me" (John 14:6, emphasis added).

Real Life Says . . .

Have you noticed that the only thing that some people cannot tolerate today is *intolerance*? The real problem with that position, of course, is that truth rests upon the conviction that some things are worthy of belief—and some aren't!

My wife and I took a cruise several years ago for our twenty-fifth wedding anniversary. We had an incredible time visiting several ports of call in the islands of the western Caribbean. Although icebergs were the furthest thing from that part of the world, we did feel a little like passengers on the *Titanic* when a harbormaster slammed our thirteen-story luxury liner into a concrete dock, delaying our return home by three days (at the cruiseline's expense!).

We went with a reputable company, but if someone had offered me a super discount rate to book our vacation with "The Royal Cruiseline of the Flat Earth Society," I would have passed on the offer. Did you know that there are still people around who believe that the earth is flat, that think that if one were to sail out toward the horizon, he would simply fall off the planet? Am I to "tolerate" that viewpoint? Certainly, if "tolerance" means allowing that person to hold his opinion, however foolish.

But to be tolerant does not mean granting equal validity to all beliefs. Just because someone somewhere believes something to be true does not *make* it true. When I believe that I should breathe oxygen, or that my car can run only on gasoline, or that New Jersey is north of where we presently live, I am not being intolerant if others hold contrary opinions. But I certainly would not want them to be my respiratory therapist, gas station attendant or travel agent!

In the Christian faith we are sometimes dealing with issues about which the Scriptures are somewhat unclear and over which Christians should charitably agree to disagree. But the fundamentals of theology should bring us to unity. As we read in Ephesians, "Make every effort to keep the unity of the Spirit through the bond of peace. There is one body and one Spirit—just as you were called to one hope when you were called—one Lord, one faith, one baptism; one God and Father of all, who is over all and through all and in all" (Ephesians 4:3-6)

But, Lord . . .

Lord, I find myself awfully intolerant toward things that don't matter, and sometimes tolerant of things contrary to Your Word. Thank You for Your grace in the midst of my mixed-up beliefs. Sharpen my discernment—and my love—for You and for others. In Jesus' name, Amen.

To Ponder . . .

In this life you sometimes have to choose between pleasing God and pleasing man. In the long run, it's better to please God—He's more apt to remember. (Harry Kemelman)

When We Trust and Obey

We demonstrate our commitment to what God has told us is true by putting His truth into practice.

It is difficult for us to believe because it is difficult for us to obey.

(Soren Kierkegaard)

Our cause is never more in danger than when a human, no longer desiring, but still intending to do our Enemy's [God's] will, looks round upon a universe from which every trace of Him seems to have vanished, and asks why he has been forsaken, and still obeys.

(Screwtape to Wormwood in
C.S. Lewis' *The Screwtape Letters*)

If anyone chooses to do God's will, he will find out whether my teaching comes from God or whether I speak on my own.

(John 7:17)

The Knowledge Nugget

Do you know anyone you would consider to be an intellectual? How would you define that term? (One jokester defined an intellectual as someone who can listen to the "William Tell Overture" without thinking of the Lone Ranger.)

Have you ever wondered why the brilliant minds of history, the intellectuals of our world, generally have not believed the gospel of Jesus Christ? For some, it may be that they have not heard a clear presentation of the gospel, or that no one has ever taken their questions seriously enough to invest the time in answering their objections. Another possibility is that the truths of the Bible and the doctrines of the Christian faith make the most sense to one whose heart and will are submitted to God. Growing in the basics of biblical faith is not just a mind thing. Perhaps some do not believe because they do not want to obey.

Marilyn vos Savant, a writer with supposedly one of the highest IQ's in the world, was asked what she believed about death. She said that pondering one's "expiration date" was useful only if it inspired one to live in this world. "Generally speaking," she said, "meditating on one's demise is a big waste of time." How foolish!

Jesus' teaching was met with skepticism because He was not in with the intellectuals of His day. He had not been formally trained as had the Jewish leaders, and we read that the Jews "were amazed and asked, 'How did this man get such learning without having studied?' " (John 7:15). Jesus responded by putting the emphasis on one's *choice* to do the will of God, and not on intellectual arguments or academic training. "My teaching is not my own. It comes from him who sent me. If anyone chooses to do God's will, he will find out whether my teaching comes from God or whether I speak on my own" (7:16-17). He then uncovered the religious leaders' plot to murder Him (7:19), confronting them with their sin. Although they thought they were keeping the law of Moses, they were actually rebelling against God's will.

Real Life Says . . .

The world around us often shouts with one voice: "It doesn't matter what you believe—as long as you don't impose your beliefs on anybody else!" Christians know it matters greatly what one believes. Our beliefs have consequences in this life and in the life to come. But beliefs are not arrived at solely through mental effort.

Is it not true that parents go through stages in raising their children? When they are young, we do not always explain *why* we ask them to do something. We want them to do as they're told because we are their parents. When they get older (especially the teenage years), they want the simplest requests defended and explained (and that's *before* they learn how to act as their own lawyers!). Sometimes God explains the why of His command, but not always. And those wanting to do His will obey because their heart and will are aligned with His. In such cases, the *mind* will soon follow. A Chinese believer once said, "I am reading the Bible now and *behaving* it." Belief and behavior go together.

But Lord . . .

Father, forgive me for disconnecting my will from my mind. Help me to long to do Your will, so that I will understand Your truth. Amen.

To Ponder . . .

Oh, the folly of any mind that would explain God before obeying Him! That would map out the character of God instead of crying, "Lord, what wouldst Thou have me to do?" (George MacDonald)

Personal (But Never Private) Piety

Today's Focus

Piety is an old word which means godliness. Our faith in Christ should make us more like our Savior—and that continuing transformation ought to be evident to others.

The more I considered Christianity, the more I found that while it had established a rule and order, the chief aim of that order was to give room for good things to run wild.

(G.K. Chesterton)

Your relationship with Christ should, by all means, be personal. But it must never be merely private!

(Carl F.H. Henry)

You are the salt of the earth. But if the salt loses its saltiness, how can it be made salty again? It is no longer good for anything, except to be thrown out and trampled by men.

You are the light of the world. A city on a hill cannot be hidden. Neither do people light a lamp and put it under a bowl. Instead they put it on its stand, and it gives light to everyone in the house. In the same way, let your light shine before men, that they may see your good deeds and praise your Father in heaven.

(Matthew 5:13-16)

The Knowledge Nugget

A lady began choking on a piece of chicken in a restaurant. An observant waiter saw her dilemma, rushed over to her and performed the Heimlich maneuver on her, saving her life. Unfortunately, he performed the maneuver incorrectly, damaging her spleen and kidney in the process. She sued him, saying, "He had no right to invade my privacy!"

Aren't you glad God has "invaded your privacy" by the gospel of Jesus Christ? A *private* kind of Christian faith says, "This is what I individually believe; it's what I need to get through life. You might believe quite differently than I do. But I certainly don't want to impose my beliefs on you!" A *personal* kind of Christian faith says, "God is not a theory to me. He is not simply the explanation for the universe; He is its almighty Creator. He has invaded my life by His truth—and His truth is there for all to receive. It is far better to 'do business' with God now than wait until you stand before His judgment!"

Private Christianity does not engage in debating the doctrines of the Christian faith. It falls victim to the pluralism of this world, which says, "All religions lead to the same mountain peak. Pick whichever one you wish!" *Personal* Christianity says, "There is only one way to the Father, and His name is Jesus Christ. All religions are not saying the same thing. The others lead not to the mountain peak, but over a cliff!"

A Christian faith that is merely private might put its greatest effort into having the right opinions about doctrine or holding the correct positions on a myriad of questions. A Christian faith that is personal does not deny the need for correct beliefs, but insists that right doctrine should lead to right behavior in a world gone terribly wrong.

Real Life Says . . .

Many in the world around us want us Christians to sit quietly in our churches, sing our hymns to each other, be nice—and leave them alone! They believe that we should be closet Christians, keeping our faith to ourselves, rather than being the salt and light in the world which Jesus commanded (Matthew 5:13-16).

In New Testament times, salt was not used for seasoning food, but for preserving it. Salt which had lost its saltiness was no longer of any value. And a light is meant to illuminate, not to be hidden! The world around us desperately needs to see that Christ has changed us, not just in the things we believe, but in the foundational ways in which we live. Of the first-century Christians it was said, "These who have turned the world upside down have come here too" (Acts 17:6, NKJV). How concerned are we about turning our world upside down?

But Lord . . .

Lord, I'm not sure I'm happy being salt and light. That means I've got a responsibility to help preserve what's right in this world and to shed the light of Your Word on what's wrong in this world. Change my will, and through me, change the world. In Jesus' name, Amen.

To Ponder . . .

We are not called to be the honey of the world but the salt of the earth. Salt stings on an open wound, but it also saves one from gangrene. (Donald Bloesch)

Hooray for Heretics?

Originally meaning a "division" or a "faction," the term *heresy* **comes from a word indicating a** *choice*. **Those who are heretics have** *chosen* **to disbelieve what the Bible teaches about some major area of Christian truth.**

Traditionally, the church has often been symbolized by an ark; those who board the ark will survive the deluge. Heresy not merely undermines one's intellectual understanding of Christian doctrine, but threatens to sink the ark, and thus to make salvation impossible for everyone, not merely for the individual heretic.

(Harold O.J. Brown)

Theology . . . is to a large extent a reaction against heresy. But heresy . . . is to a large extent a response to truth.

(Harold O.J. Brown)

Timothy, guard what has been entrusted to your care. Turn away from godless chatter and the opposing ideas of what is falsely called knowledge, which some have professed and in so doing have wandered from the faith.

(1 Timothy 6:20-21)

The Knowledge Nugget

In the early church the believers diligently gave themselves to preaching the gospel in obedience to Jesus' command in Matthew 28:19-20: "Go and make disciples of all nations, baptizing them in the name of the Father and of the Son and of the Holy Spirit, and teaching them to obey everything I have commanded you." We call this mandate the Great Commission.

But how did the early church react when some came along and questioned the doctrine of Christ's deity? Or the personality of the Holy Spirit? Or the genuineness of the Son's humanity? Or salvation by grace alone? Those who challenged orthodoxy in the first few centuries (and their present-day descendants, such as the Jehovah's Witnesses, Mormons, etc.) were called "heretics," a word basically meaning "party" or "sect."

The term can also refer to "choice," in the sense that one truth is emphasized to the exclusion of others. The Jehovah's Witnesses, for example, are adamant *monotheists*; they insist that there is only one God, just as Christians do, but they emphasize it to the exclusion of any idea of the Trinity. Regardless of the biblical indications of a plurality in the Godhead, these modern-day heretics spread a "gospel" that teaches that the Son was created by Jehovah, and therefore is less than divine. They are repeating a false teaching made popular by Arius, a fourth-century presbyter who was condemned by the Nicene Creed (325 A.D.).

When heretics came along in the early church, believers had to devote themselves to thinking through their faith in order to combat false teaching, prepare young Christians to defend biblical orthodoxy and be obedient to Paul's call to vigilance in such passages as First Timothy 6:20: "guard what has been entrusted to your care." Theologians such as Irenaeus, Tertullian and Augustine wrote volumes defending biblical truth, providing leadership in the development of our early confessions and creeds.

Although we should never be thankful for error, heretics have forced Christians to hammer out genuine orthodoxy. The downside of heresy is that it preaches a false gospel which will not save, deters people from the Word of God and divides Christians from one another. Such ideas "promote controversies rather than God's work—which is by faith" (1:4).

Real Life Says . . .

For most people outside Christian circles, there is no absolute truth which must be defended. For them "heresy" is a worn-out, judgmental term which should be retired, for it conjures up images of people being burned at the stake "for their opinions." Although we cannot and should not defend the mistreatment of heretics in church history, we must take the Bible seriously when it warns us that false ideas about God and His truth will spiritually injure those for whom Christ died.

Let's say a hospital patient is examined by two doctors, one who recommends oxygen, the other carbon monoxide! The first doctor's recommendation will help the patient; the second's will bring death. How is it that when it comes to religious ideas, we act as if all opinions were on the level of life-giving oxygen? Some ideas will lead to spiritual suffocation!

But Lord . . .

Father, I know that there are many challenges to Your truth in this world. Help me so to grasp Your Word that I recognize when I am straying, so that I can help others who wander from sound doctrine. In Jesus' name, Amen.

To Ponder . . .

Good health is not contagious, but bad health is. (Neil Anderson)

Beware of Philosophy!

Originally meaning "the love of wisdom," philosophy is seen by many Christians as an enemy of Christian faith. It need not necessarily be.

The society which scorns excellence in plumbing because plumbing is a humble activity, and tolerates shoddiness in philosophy because it is an exalted activity, will have neither good plumbing nor good philosophy. Neither its pipes nor its theories will hold water.

(John Gardner)

Philosophy accepts the hard and hazardous task of dealing with problems not yet open to the methods of science—problems like good and evil, beauty and ugliness, order and freedom, life and death.

(Will Durant)

See to it that no one takes you captive through hollow and deceptive philosophy, which depends on human tradition and the basic principles of this world rather than on Christ.

(Colossians 2:8)

The Knowledge Nugget

Philosophy is supposed to be "the love of wisdom," but so often it seems to be a strong affection for foolishness! Someone has said that if you were in an elevator with a good philosopher, he could use arguments that would make you doubt your very existence—and then you would probably miss your floor!

In many ways, however, philosophy can actually help, not hinder, the study of doctrine. A philosophy which recognizes the final authority of the Word of God can help us analyze and confront heretical thought systems. The early Church used Christian philosophy to take a stand against heresies like Docetism (a worldview which cast doubt on the humanity of Christ), gnosticism (a movement which claimed to have "secret knowledge" [*gnosis* means "to know"] from Jesus, and that one's faith was incomplete without it) and stoicism (a philosophy that emphasized the power of destiny and denied the immortality of the human soul). A philosophy which is consistent with the Word of God will help us face similar challenges to God's truth today.

Real Life Says . . .

We are not to let men "[take us] captive by hollow and deceptive philosophy." But if philosophy helps us to think properly and to understand worldviews and thought systems, then it can indeed be theology's "handmaiden." The Apostle Paul tells us that it is "hollow and deceptive philosophy" against which we should guard ourselves.

The Three Stooges—Larry, Moe and Curly—all applied for a bookkeeping job. "This is impossible," said the boss. "I can't hire all three of you. Besides, none of you look like you even got past the third grade." But the three wouldn't relent until finally, exasperated, the boss said, "OK! If you can answer a simple question, I'll give you the job." He turned to Larry and said, "What's three times three?"

Larry started counting on his fingers. "Let's see . . . 3, 7, 19, 35 . . . Is it *128*?"

The boss shook his head and turned to Moe. "What's three times three?"

Moe immediately shouted, "WEDNESDAY!"

The boss, beginning to become disgusted, turned to Curly. "What's three times three?"

He thought for a moment and then asked for a pencil and a piece of paper. After writing furiously for some time, Curly finally looked up and said, "Nine."

The boss was amazed and, true to his word, he began filling out the employment papers. As he was writing, he said, "This is incredible! I thought you were a complete moron! How did you do it?"

Curly responded, "Oh, it was easy. I divided 128 by Wednesday!"

Every human being has a philosophy of life—a way of providing *answers* to life's problems. However, the Bible teaches that "there is a way that seems right to a man, but in the end it leads to death" (Proverbs 14:12). The follower of Jesus Christ also has a way of looking at the world, a philosophy. Growing strong in the doctrines of biblical Christianity will protect the believer from falling captive to "hollow and deceptive philosophy" (Colossians 2:8). And knowing God's truth will lead to a love of true wisdom.

But, Lord . . .

Lord, I know I need to learn to think more clearly. And sometimes that involves learning some philosophy. Help me to love Your wisdom today! In Jesus' name, Amen.

To Ponder . . .

Everyone has a philosophy about life. But if a person doesn't have Christ, that person doesn't have the wisdom of God, and all that's left is the hollow and deceptive foolishness of this world.

Have Ye Not Read?

In order to understand the truths of the Christian faith, the follower of Jesus Christ must be an avid reader. There is no substitute for consistent and careful reading.

If God is a reality, and the soul is a reality, and you are an immortal being, what are you doing with your Bible shut?

(Herrick Johnson)

It cannot be that the people should grow in grace unless they give themselves to reading. A reading people will always be a knowing people. A people who talk much will know little.

(John Wesley)

On one occasion an expert in the law stood up to test Jesus. "Teacher," he asked, "what must I do to inherit eternal life?"

"What is written in the Law?" He replied. "How do you read it?"

(Luke 10:25-26)

The Knowledge Nugget

The science fiction writer Ray Bradbury once said, "You don't have to burn books to destroy a culture. Just get people to stop reading them." If the Christian faith is primarily communicated to us in a book (the Bible), then there is no substitute for personally reading that book over and over again. It is not necessary for the Bible to be burned for our Christian faith to be destroyed. All that needs to happen is for Christians to stop reading the Word of God.

How do we best grow in our understanding of the biblical faith? We may listen to sound teachers and preachers dispensing the fruit of their studies. Christian videos and tapes may advance us in our grasp of godliness. But there is no substitute for the personal reading and research of the Word of God in the life of the child of God. According to Russell Chandler in his book *Racing Toward 2001*, there are estimated to be between 23 million and 60 million U.S. adults who are functionally illiterate. One study indicated that sixty-one percent of all seventeen-year-olds can't read their high school textbooks. Reading is fundamental to understanding God's ways in the world.

The Living Word of God, the Lord Jesus, asked the question, "Have you not read?" on five occasions:

1. When His disciples were being criticized by the Pharisees for eating grain on the Sabbath, Jesus responded: "Haven't you read what David did when he and his companions were hungry?" (Matthew 12:3), referring back to First Samuel 21. Two verses later (Matthew 12:5), Jesus repeated His question: "Haven't you read in the Law that on the Sabbath the priests in the temple desecrate the day and yet are innocent?" which is a reference to Numbers 28.

2. In Matthew 19 Jesus answered the Pharisees' test concerning the thorny issue of divorce. He asked, "Haven't you read . . . that at the beginning the Creator 'made them male and female' . . . ?" (19:4), referring back to the very first chapter of the first book of the Bible, Genesis.

3. On one occasion the religious leaders heard the children praising Jesus in the temple and they became indignant. Jesus responded, "Have you never read, 'From the lips of children and infants you have ordained praise'?" (21:16, a reference to Psalm 8:2).

4. In a confrontation with the Sadducees about the issue of the resurrection, Jesus minced no words when He said, "Now about the dead rising—have you not read in the book of Moses, in the account of the bush, how God said to him, 'I am the God of Abraham, the God of Isaac, and the God of Jacob'? He is not the God of the dead, but of the living. You are badly mistaken!" (Mark 12:26-27). It's bad enough to be mistaken, but even worse to be *badly* mistaken!

5. In Mark 12 Jesus countered the rejection of Israel's religious leaders by asking, "Haven't you read this scripture: 'The stone the builders rejected has become the capstone; the Lord has done this, and it is marvelous in our eyes'?" (12:10-11), a reference to the prophecy of Psalm 118:22-23.

Real Life Says . . .

"Read for pleasure," says our world, "or read to advance in your occupation. But don't let anyone—especially a *book*—tell you what to think!" But if reading is to the mind what exercise is to the body, then the believer in Jesus Christ must do his calisthenics. And God has revealed His will and His mind precisely in a book.

But Lord . . .

Father, thank You for Your Word. Give me discipline—and joy—in the reading of it. And help me to believe what I read. In Jesus' name, Amen.

To Ponder . . .

A book, shut tight, is but a block of paper. (Chinese proverb)

The Power of a Bad Example

The study of how both believers and unbelievers have understood the truths of God (a basic definition of "historical theology") teaches us what errors we should avoid in living the life of faith.

Few things are harder to put up with than the annoyance of a good example.

(Mark Twain)

God has no more precious gift to a church or an age than a man who lives as an embodiment of His will, and inspires those around him with the faith of what grace can do.

(Andrew Murray)

Don't let anyone look down on you because you are young, but set an example for the believers in speech, in life, in love, in faith and in purity. Until I come, devote yourself to the public reading of Scripture, to preaching and to teaching.

(1 Timothy 4:12-13)

The Knowledge Nugget

In the fifth century A.D. Simeon Stylites dedicated himself as a teenager to pursuing God through meditation, prayer and mortification (turning away from the most basic of human pleasures). History tells us that he ate only once a week, lived on a mountain as a hermit and fastened a heavy iron chain upon his feet, believing that these acts would bring him closer to God.

Still unsatisfied with his life, Simeon pursued a new kind of holiness in 423 when he climbed to the top of a pillar and lived there for thirty-six years! *He never came down.* The pillar (designed so that he could not lie down) grew in height until it eventually reached sixty feet. He could only stand or lean against a banister. He would spend his days genuflecting (bowing) before God. One spectator counted 1,244 such genuflexions in one day. Exposed to the elements, Simeon would stand, praying and preaching penance for sin. Many people sought his counsel. In fact, the two important church conferences held at Ephesus (431) and Chalcedon (451) sought the illiterate Simeon's blessing on their deliberations. Simeon's style of spirituality produced the "pillar hermit," a class of revered individuals that lasted for twelve centuries!

Real Life Says . . .

The world around us looks at a person like Simeon and says he was crazy. And perhaps he was. His effort to escape the world (and its inhabitants) does not seem to square with statements made by Jesus such as John 17:15: "My prayer is not that you take them out of the world but that you protect them from the evil one" or Matthew 5:16: "Let your light shine before men, that they may see your good deeds and praise your Father in heaven."

But before we judge Simeon too harshly, we should note that his radical kind of Christianity demonstrated a profound sense of personal sin and a longing to eventually attain the holiness "without [which] no one will see the Lord" (Hebrews 12:14). Simeon's asceticism (denying God-given bodily needs and pleasures) failed to reflect the biblical truth that we belong to a God "who richly provides us with everything for our enjoyment" (1 Timothy 6:17). But in our materialistic, overindulgent society, we need the shocking contrast of a Simeon who gave up worldly pleasures for what he thought to be the will of God.

People around us might look at Simeon and say that his life shows that the only way to find peace with God is by one's superhuman efforts at self-denial and sacrifice. And that is truly sad, for it is missing the gospel of grace which is offered as God's gift, impossible for anyone to earn by any human means.

The Apostle Paul does not advise Timothy to go live high up on a pillar, separated from the world for which Christ died. Instead, he admonishes him not to "let anyone look down on you because you are young, but set an example for the believers in speech, in life, in love, in faith and in purity. Until I come, devote yourself to the public reading of Scripture, to preaching and to teaching" (4:12-13). Such a life, dedicated to godly communication, conduct, compassion, conviction and consecration, demonstrates the life-changing grace of God. And that's an example worth following!

But Lord . . .

Lord, sometimes I would prefer the top of such a pillar instead of life on this sinful sphere. Help me to serve You today among those for whom You died. In Jesus' name, Amen.

To Ponder . . .

There is no power on earth that can neutralize the influence of a high, simple and useful life. (Booker T. Washington)

An Orthodox Rebel

A term meaning "right praise," to be "orthodox" involves living life in such a way that our behavior and our beliefs are consistent with the Word of God.

Cold, hard orthodoxy can sometimes be the reflection of a cold, hard heart.

(Stephen Brown)

When it comes to theology, it is possible to be as straight as a gun barrel—and just as empty.

(George Murray)

I am a Hebrew and I worship the LORD, the God of heaven, who made the sea and the land. . . . I knew that you are a gracious and compassionate God, slow to anger and abounding in love, a God who relents from sending calamity.

(Jonah 1:9, 4:2)

The Knowledge Nugget

We have seen in our studies that most of us believe far more than we behave. However, as we grow in our grasp of the basics of biblical Christianity, it is quite possible to be orthodox in what we believe, but heretical in how we behave.

Perhaps there is no better example of this contradiction than the runaway missionary Jonah. Commanded by God to preach to the Ninevites, he chose to flee from God instead, going in the opposite direction. God sent a storm which threatened to sink Jonah's escape vessel. The pagan sailors woke Jonah up to get him to join their ecumenical prayer meeting, hoping that maybe his god would be the one to save them. After determining that Jonah was the reason for the storm, they insisted he identify himself. He proclaimed: "I am a Hebrew and I worship the LORD, the God of heaven, who made the sea and the land" (Jonah 1:9).

Of course, he was *not* worshiping the Lord as he spoke those words, for he was in active rebellion against God's will. The only way the storm could be calmed was for Jonah to be hurled overboard, an action the pagan sailors took with great reluctance. In fact, they pleaded that Jonah's God not hold this action against them! It appears that they were converted to the true God during this time (despite Jonah's witness, not because of it), for we read that "the men greatly feared the LORD, and they offered a sacrifice to the LORD and made vows to him" (1:16). God is able to convert all who come to Him, even when His disobedient messengers get in the way!

We're all familiar with the story of Jonah being swallowed by a great sea creature which was specially provided for that occasion. (The Bible does not say that it was a whale.) Jonah's orthodoxy is further shown by his prayer from inside the sea creature! That prayer (in chapter 2) contains the excellent declaration: "Salvation comes from the LORD" (2:9).

Jonah finally does God's will, which involved preaching God's judgment to the people of Nineveh. His message was brief: "Forty more days and Nineveh will be overturned" (3:4). I think Jonah probably learned only enough Assyrian to speak those seven words. He didn't want the Ninevites to be saved.

But the Ninevites repented and, instead of celebrating God's mercy, Jonah threw a huge temper tantrum! Yet even in his anger, he spoke of God's attribute of forgiveness: "You are a gracious and compassionate God, slow to anger and abounding in love, a God who relents from sending calamity" (4:2).

Real Life Says . . .

For many today the discrepancy between what they believe and how they act is of little concern. At long as one "does his job" and doesn't hurt anyone, the contradiction between one's lips and one's life seems largely irrelevant.

In Jonah's case, he missed the blessing of willingly doing God's work. His own rebellion had blinded him to the fact of his *own* forgiveness. And, in the end, he cared more about personal comfort than he did about the lost condition of others. Rebelling against God's truth will do that to a heart.

In his book *You! Jonah!* Thomas John Carlisle shows the contradiction between Jonah's belief and his obedience in the poem "Negotiation with a Higher Power": "I will demonstrate my immediate obedience, providing You comply with my demand for a more satisfying assignment."

Is that the condition of your obedience?

But Lord . . .

Father, I thank You for Your mercy to me. Help me to show by my obedience the truth of my heart, and enlarge my heart to care that others come to know You. In Jesus' name, Amen.

To Ponder . . .

Delayed obedience is always disobedience.

Do You Feel the Need for a Creed?

A creed or confession provides a brief statement of some key truths of biblical faith.

A faith in God that does not want to be questioned and shrinks from being examined by outsiders is a faith that does not wish to be shared. It draws a circle close and tight around itself. Its creeds, rituals and teachings become protective devices against the world's intruding curiosity. Thus it proves that it is something less than faith—it is pride, defensiveness, fear of being found out by the truth.

(Roger Hazelton)

It is said that a very cautious clergyman in Detroit once challenged his congregation with these words: "Dearly beloved, unless you repent of your sins in a measure, and become converted in a degree, you will, I regret to say, be damned to a more or less extent."

Beyond all question, the mystery of godliness is great:

He appeared in a body,
 was vindicated by the Spirit,
was seen by angels,
 was preached among the nations,

was believed on in the world,
was taken up in glory.

(1 Timothy 3:16)

The Knowledge Nugget

Christian orthodoxy has produced several confessions and creeds, and those carefully crafted statements of Christian faith can be both helpful and dangerous. Their help lies in their clarity and brevity of expression; their danger lies in the fact that they must not take the place of the Bible, the Word of God, as the final authority for the Christian.

We need to be thankful for those throughout church history who worked hard to craft doctrinal statements to combat heresy, train new converts and summarize the important issues of the Christian faith. Some of those creeds are brief and simple (the Apostles' Creed, for example), while others are lengthy and technical (such as the Chalcedonian Creed). But creeds and confessional statements are needed by the church and useful in highlighting the fundamentals of the faith.

A creed, however, is not synonymous with Scripture. Some creeds may focus on a particular doctrine or emphasize a belief that is not a major doctrine (as we will see in one of our devotionals on the doctrine of Christ).

When the Apostle Paul writes: "Beyond all question, the mystery of godliness is great: He appeared in a body, was vindicated by the Spirit, was seen by angels, was preached among the nations, was believed on in the world, was taken up in glory" (3:16), he is giving an early doctrinal confession for Christians. These six theological affirmations are central to Christian faith. We must affirm the true humanity of the Lord Jesus ("appeared in a body"), His bodily resurrection ("was vindicated by the Spirit"), His superiority to the angelic world ("was seen by angels"), His central place in the focus of the gospel ("was preached among the nations"), His worthiness of our faith ("was believed on in the world") and His ascension ("was taken up in glory"). But this early creedal statement says nothing about the authority of the Bible, the existence of God as a Trinity or a specific view of the atoning work of Christ. However, its six compact declarations about Christ direct our attention to His person and His centrality to living faith. And for that we should be most grateful!

Real Life Says . . .

The world's focus is not on *what* one believes, but on what one *feels* about what one believes or on the issue of *respecting others* of differing beliefs. Because many in our society do not accept the concept of absolute truth, creeds and confessional statements make little sense to them.

The noted skeptic and atheistic philosopher Bertrand Russell was once asked, "Would you be willing to die for any of your beliefs?" He quickly responded, "Of course not. I might be wrong!" Is there no truth that stands above us, which gives us a certainty about life—and death? Christian creeds and confessions emphasize that the real God has disclosed to us what is ultimately and finally true in this universe. And those matters are of eternal significance!

But Lord . . .

Lord, some of us come from churches that recite creeds and some of us don't. May our recitations not become rote and meaningless, nor may our failure to confess our doctrine leave our hearts cold or our minds unsure of Your grace in our lives. In Jesus' name, Amen.

To Ponder . . .

If someone had to compose a Christian creed based upon your life, what would they write?

The individual Christian must take personal responsibility for growth in the truths of God, rather than blaming circumstances—or others.

We cannot become what we need to be by remaining what we are.

(Max De Pree)

Faith is like the little boy who tied a rope swing onto a sapling's branch. Then, noticing that the seat of the swing rested on the ground, he got a garden hose and watered the sapling.

But to each one of us grace has been given. . . . So that the body of Christ may be built up. . . .

[And] we will no longer be infants, tossed back and forth by the waves, and blown here and there by every wind of teaching and by the cunning and craftiness of men in their deceitful scheming. Instead, speaking the truth in love, we will in all things grow up into him who is the Head, that is, Christ.

(Ephesians 4:7, 12, 14-15).

The Knowledge Nugget

The doctrines of the Bible have been given that we might be brought into conformity with God's reality (Titus 2:11-14), that we might be equipped for helping others (2 Timothy 3:16-17) and that we might become strong in our faith (Ephesians 4:12-15). Instead of being an anchorless raft on a storm-tossed sea or a runaway kite which is no longer tethered to the earth, the believer in Christ is to be grounded in God's truth.

One of my best friends tells about buying a large, expensive kite that he could fly with his sons. On the prairies of Manitoba, Canada, the winds can whip up quickly. Dean had his youngest son Stefen holding onto the kite when a strong wind came without warning. He yelled, "Hold on!", not wanting to lose the expensive kite. His son Stefen held on so tightly that he was raised *off the ground* by the wind and had to be rescued by his father. When Stefen became a teenager, Dean wondered if he had done the right thing!

God has given us His Word that we might be grounded—or, as Paul puts it, "renewed in knowledge in the image of its Creator" (Colossians 3:10). God's Word presents a program to the Christian for growth in godliness; advancement in God's truth involves putting into practice what the believer learns.

Real Life Says . . .

Some in our world try to blame everyone but themselves for their mistakes and failures. The late Erma Bombeck once wrote, "Women no longer take the blame for ring-around-the-collar, but place the blame where it belongs—on men who don't wash their necks!" Believers in Christ also suffer from a kind of victim mentality: "My pastor wasn't a very good preacher . . ."; "I attended a really dead church. . . ." The Bible is quite clear that we are to take responsibility for our own Christian growth.

In his excellent book *The Gospel of Coincidence*, John Boykin critiques the viewpoint that we are helpless victims in decision-making and argues that our life consists of the choices we make. "My favorite absurdity," he says, "comes from a renowned historian who, describing the origins of World War I, wrote that 'planning for war assumed its own momentum until 1914 military expediency dominated the decision-making process, and war declared itself'." We know that war does not declare itself. People make decisions. We are responsible for the choices we make in our lives.

You and I can make the choice to water that sapling for ourselves. Just as a tree needs water to grow, so our lives need the nourishment of God's Word.

But Lord . . .

Father, I don't want to be tossed back and forth or blown here and there by ideas inconsistent with Your truth. Help me to make the kinds of choices which will strengthen my faith for Your sake . . . and for mine. In Jesus' name, Amen.

To Ponder . . .

The following is apparently from a young believer in Zimbabwe who was later martyred for his faith: "I'm part of the fellowship of the unashamed. I have the power of the Holy Spirit. The die has been cast. I have stepped over the line. The decision has been made—I'm a disciple of Jesus. I won't look back, let up, slow down, back away, or be still. My past is redeemed, my present makes sense, my future is secure. I'm finished and done now with low living, sight walking, smooth knees, colorless dreams, tamed visions, worldly talking, cheap giving and dwarfed goals."

Don't Hitchhike!

Today's Focus

To grow strong in the truths of God, we need to learn from other believers, but we must walk the Christian walk on our own.

Someone has said, "Before you criticize a man, walk a mile in his shoes. That way, if he gets angry, he's a mile away and barefoot!"

The existentialist philosopher Soren Kierkegaard once wrote to his hypochondriac niece: "Above all, do not lose your desire to walk; every day I walk myself into a state of well-being and walk away from every illness; I have walked myself into my best thoughts, and I know of no thought so burdensome that one cannot walk away from it."

(Letters and Documents)

O people of Zion, who live in Jerusalem, you will weep no more. How gracious he will be when you cry for help! As soon as he hears, he will answer you.... Whether you turn to the right or to the left, your ears will hear a voice behind you, saying, "This is the way; walk in it."

(Isaiah 30:19, 21)

The Knowledge Nugget

One morning, I dropped my car off to be repaired and faced a choice. I could either wait for it in the repair shop's "sensory deprivation chamber" (have you had to watch daytime TV recently?) or I could walk the two miles home and pick up the car later. I chose to walk and I found myself thinking about—theology!

I learned that walking on the right shoulder of the road home was a matter of faith. With my back to the cars, I had to believe that people driving to work would drink their coffee or apply their make-up *very* carefully as they steered their vehicles at (what seemed to me to be) 200 miles an hour behind me!

I also learned that at any moment I could choose to stop walking, stick out my thumb and start hitchhiking. No doubt someone would have taken pity on me, picked me up and deposited me very near my house. But I decided to walk—the whole two miles—uphill (well, some of it was uphill).

Is it possible that many of us hitchhike on what others *believe*? They have thought through their faith by studying the Bible, and have either written or preached those truths in an engaging fashion. We stick out our spiritual thumbs and wait to be picked up and deposited at the doorstep of our eternal home.

When Paul says to the Philippians that they ought to "continue to work out [their] salvation with fear and trembling" (Philippians 2:12), he is complimenting them for their initial progress in spiritual things. He implies that they—and we—*could* stop moving ahead in the truths of God, and therefore need to "continue to work out" the implications of our faith. Lest anyone think that he can advance in godliness without God's strength at every point, Paul adds, "for it is God who works in you to will and to act according to his good purpose" (2:13).

Real Life Says . . .

The world around us does not encourage us to hammer out our own biblical understanding of our faith. With its addiction to celebrities and their often sad lives, it indoctrinates us into fantasy living (note the appeal of soap operas and so-called reality shows). We might be led to believe, even in Christian circles, that growing in our faith is something we should entrust to the "experts" who interpret the Bible for us. Although we need solid teaching from the Word, the burden is on the individual believer to advance in godliness through an ever-increasing attention to the truths of God's Word.

Real Christianity teaches that God has revealed His mind and heart to His people through His Word, the Bible. And the Bible is far more than a tourist map! It is a detailed guidebook about ourselves (the travelers), our Guide (the Lord Jesus) and our destination (heaven). In the walk of faith, there is no room on the highway of life for spiritual hitchhikers!

But Lord . . .

Father, forgive me when I act like a spiritual two-year-old who wants to be carried everywhere. By Your Spirit develop a strength in me that will give me the power to walk strong in Your truth today. In Christ's name, Amen.

To Ponder . . .

The spiritual journey is best pursued by walkers, not by loiterers or hitchhikers.

The Right Rites

We express our Christian beliefs through certain practices ("rites" or "rituals") which must always be tested by the teaching of the Word. When a practice or custom loses its biblical meaning, it must be reexamined, renewed or replaced.

When Christian worship is dull and joyless, Jesus Christ has been left outside—that is the only possible explanation.

(James S. Stewart)

First you have a reality, then you have a response to the reality. Thirdly, you have a repetition of the response to the reality. And then you have a repetition without a reality.

(Stephen Brown)

"The multitude of your sacrifices—
    what are they to me?" says the LORD.
"I have more than enough of burnt offerings,
    of rams and the fat of fattened animals;
I have no pleasure
        in the blood of bulls and lambs and goats.
When you come to appear before me,
    who has asked this of you,
        this trampling of my courts?

Stop bringing meaningless offerings!
    Your incense is detestable to me.
New Moons, Sabbaths and convocations—
    I cannot bear your evil assemblies."

(Isaiah 1:11-13)

The Knowledge Nugget

A Lutheran magazine described a very unusual recessional that took place at the conclusion of a Sunday morning service in an Ontario church. The choir began singing as they marched in perfect unison up the center aisle to the back of the church. The last young lady in the women's section was wearing a new pair of shoes with thin heels. She stepped on the grating that covered the hot air register in the church, and her heel stuck. Knowing that she couldn't hold up the recessional, she simply slipped her foot out of the shoe and kept on marching without missing a beat. There wasn't a break at all; everything moved like clockwork. The first man following the young woman noted the situation, reached down and picked up her shoe. The entire grate came up with it. Startled, but still singing, the man continued up the aisle, bearing in his hand the grate, attached to the shoe. There was never a break in the recessional; everybody was singing and everything moved like clockwork—until the next man, still singing, stepped into the open register and disappeared!

Have you ever felt that way? Are we sometimes guilty of just "keeping the machinery going" instead of worshiping the Lord with meaning and intimacy?

For the people of Israel, the problem was that the rites, the rituals which they practiced, had lost connection to the reality they were supposed to reflect. In Isaiah 1, God essentially says that He is sick of their meaningless sacrifices, of their complicated (and noisy) "trampling of my courts." (And it was the Lord who had initiated those ceremonies!) They had lost the reality of why they did what they did.

Real Life Says . . .

Modern men and women do not want to be told how they are to worship God. We *Christians* sometimes act as if the way we do things in our churches can never be improved or replaced. When we become more concerned with defending the way we do things than with the meaning of the things we do, we are committing the same error as the Israelites. Ceremonies without significance, rituals without reality, religious practices which have lost their purpose, are all repugnant to God!

The musician Greg Voltz expresses reality-disconnected rituals when he sings:

> We sit for the preacher and he lulls us to sleep;
> We're under the stupor of the regimen we keep;
> The routine is comforting; don't want to face the
>   unknown;
> But we give up our shot at the freedom we're shown.

The Bible gives us tremendous freedom in developing practices which communicate God's truth. But we must learn from Israel's failure to worship the Lord "in spirit and in truth, for they are the kind of worshipers the Father seeks" (John 4:23).

But Lord . . .

Father, it is so easy for me to become attached to the religious things that I do, instead of to You. Thank You for the tangible ways I can worship You. Help me always to test them by Your Word. In Jesus' name, Amen.

To Ponder . . .

A rite which does not communicate God and His Word is not right; it is wrong!

What the World Needs Now

The final defense (or "apologetic") of the truths of biblical Christianity is not our clever arguments, but our committed love of one another.

Alexander, Caesar and Hannibal conquered the world but they had no friends. . . . Jesus founded his empire upon love, and at this hour millions would die for him. . . . He has won the hearts of men, a task a conqueror cannot do.

(Napoleon Bonaparte)

Take away love, and our earth is a tomb.

(Robert Browning)

A new command I give you: Love one another. As I have loved you, so you must love one another. By this all men will know that you are my disciples, if you love one another.

(John 13:34-35)

The Knowledge Nugget

Much has been said in these devotionals about proper belief. We need to be good theologians who love God and His truth. The Christian faith is a definite content of truths which we should embrace and defend. We must take personal responsibility for our growth in godliness, and that involves the engagement of our minds with the Word of God, the Bible.

Someone has said, "You don't win people by winning arguments." There is some truth to that statement; however, as someone else has said, "You won't win anyone if you lose all the arguments!" We are not to be argumentative as Christians, but we must know what we believe so that we can give an answer for the hope which we have in Jesus Christ (1 Peter 3:15).

More people look at our lives than debate our doctrines. Therefore we need to listen to Jesus' challenge in John 13 to "love one another." Paul wrote to the Philippians that they were to "stand firm in one spirit, contending as one man for the faith of the gospel" (Philippians 1:27). In fact, the great apostle said that the love of the Philippians for one another truly mattered to him: "Make my joy complete by being like-minded, having the same love, being one in spirit and purpose" (2:2).

Real Life Says . . .

The world around us often looks upon our churches with confusion. We say that we have experienced the love of God, but our hearts that go out to God in praise hardly go across the pews to God's people in love. The world longs to see visible evidence of God's care for broken people, and His means of showing that care is through His people.

When the love of God, which has been "shed abroad in our hearts" (Romans 5:5, KJV), is spread among the people of God, a love-starved world will pay attention. The same writer who recorded the challenge of Jesus to His disciples to love one another in John 13 continued that theme in First John. There we read verses such as: "How great is the love the Father has lavished on us, that we should be called the children of God! And that is what we are!" (1 John 3:1); "We know that we have passed from death to life, because we love our brothers" (3:14); "This is how we know what love is: Jesus Christ laid down his life for us. And we ought to lay down our lives for our brothers" (3:16); "This is his command: to believe in the name of his Son, Jesus Christ, and to love one another as he commanded us" (3:23); "This is love: not that we loved God, but that he loved us and sent his Son as an atoning sacrifice for our sins. Dear friends, since God so loved us, we also ought to love one another" (4:10-11). Any questions?

The story is told of a man who was visiting his friend who worked as a security guard in a maximum security mental hospital. "Bill," said the man, "from what I can see there are only three security guards on duty here—and over a hundred violent patients! Aren't you afraid they'll revolt?"

"Not at all," Bill responded. "Lunatics never unite."

But Lord . . .

Father, I know that I can focus on my love for You and forget to love Your children. Help me to see that the world has the right to judge whether I am Your disciple by the love I have for Your people. In Jesus' name, Amen.

To Ponder . . .

How much you love the God you cannot see is shown by your love for His children whom you can see.

The Power of Biblical Unity

Biblical unity in the faith involves demonstrating oneness in the essentials and charity in the nonessentials.

Talk about what you believe and you have disunity. Talk about Who you believe in and you have unity.

(E. Stanley Jones)

We must all learn to live together as brothers or we will perish together as fools.

(Martin Luther King, Jr.)

It was he who gave some to be apostles, some to be prophets, some to be evangelists, and some to be pastors and teachers, to prepare God's people for works of service, so that the body of Christ may be built up until we all reach unity in the faith and in the knowledge of the Son of God and become mature, attaining to the whole measure of the fullness of Christ.

(Ephesians 4:11-13)

The Knowledge Nugget

We saw in Day 17 that Jesus challenged His disciples with the words: "As I have loved you, so you must love one another. By this all men will know that you are my disciples, if you love one another" (John 13:34-35). That "final apologetic" of love does not take the place of the essential doctrines of the faith; it demonstrates their reality to a watching world.

Biblical unity, as we see in the book of Ephesians, is both a status to be maintained ("Make every effort to keep the unity of the Spirit through the bond of peace," Ephesians 4:3) and a goal to be achieved ("until we all reach unity in the faith and in the knowledge of the Son of God," Ephesians 4:13). We destroy that unity when we confuse our *distinctive* areas of doctrine (such as our view of the mode of baptism, or the type of church government, or whether Jesus is coming back for His Church before or after the tribulation) with the *essential* truths of the Christian faith.

In describing an international conference of the World Council of Churches held in the early 1960s, Malcolm Muggeridge, who late in his life became a defender of Christian orthodoxy, wrote, "They were able to agree about almost anything, because they believed almost nothing." Unity at the cost of Christianity's fundamentals is not biblical unity.

As we see in Ephesians 4, God has given us all we need for achieving biblical unity by providing apostles, prophets, evangelists, pastors and teachers. Their job is to equip God's people to do God's work. The purpose of all the people of God being mobilized in ministry is "so that the body of Christ may be built up" (4:12). As each believer exercises his gift(s) for the building up of the body, an observable unity should be manifested as the church matures.

Real Life Says . . .

The world around us wastes no time attacking Christians when a church has split or believers are not getting along with one another. When a group of God's people really believes the same things (the essentials of the faith) and demonstrates a visible oneness in their love for each another, the world will sit up and take notice. In a world fragmented and torn apart by a multitude of causes and opinions, the belief-enriched unity of the church is a powerful witness to the reality of the true God.

An Australian newspaper reporter tells about interviewing Isaac Stern, the famous violinist: "He was rehearsing Bach's E Major Concerto when I asked him how things were going. 'Well,' he said, 'I've got wonderful music, a wonderful violin and a wonderful bow. All I've got to do is let them get together—and not get in their way.' "

For the believer in Jesus Christ, our musical "score" is the faith which has been "once for all delivered to the saints" (Jude 3, NKJV). We each have a part to play. Our responsibility is to pay close attention to that score and to play it together, with joy, before a listening world.

But Lord . . .

Father, Great Musician of my life, so tune my heart that I will not strive to play solo, nor act as if the other members of Your orchestra are unnecessary. Forgive me when I seek to edit Your composition. Help me to follow Your conducting of my life. In Jesus' name, Amen.

To Ponder . . .

If we follow God's score, the world will listen to the music He makes through our lives.

Sacred Cows Make Gourmet Burgers!

Today's Focus

The regular practices of believers gathered together must be evaluated by the Word of God.

Tradition is the living faith of those now dead; traditionalism is the dead faith of those still living.

(Jaroslav Pelikan)

[Tradition is] an extension of the franchise . . . giving votes to that most obscure of all classes, our ancestors.

(G.K. Chesterton)

Some Pharisees and teachers of the law . . . asked, "Why do your disciples break the tradition of the elders? They don't wash their hands before they eat!"

Jesus replied, "And why do you break the command of God for the sake of your tradition?"

(Matthew 15:1-3)

The Knowledge Nugget

Howard Hendricks, the retired master teacher from Dallas Theological Seminary, tells about a church he visited not too long ago. "This church has the finest program for 1946 you have ever seen. It's just unfortunate they weren't in 1946. If they were, they're loaded for bear. They were telling me about the problems they were having with their finances. When I met with them to evaluate it, I said, 'I've got a solution for your financial problems.' 'Oh, really? What is it, doctor?' I said, 'I suggest you build a fence around this church and then charge admission for people to come in and see what it was like in the last generation.' "

As we saw in our devotional for Day 16 ("The Right Rites"), the development of traditions and rituals can be a blessing of God. Such practices help to formalize what we believe and, to the degree that they reflect biblical doctrine and communicate it clearly, can assist the church in passing on God's truth to succeeding generations.

The problem with traditions is that they may lose their meaning or, worse yet, they may replace the Word of God rather than communicate it. The latter is precisely what happened to the Jews in Jesus' day. Because Jesus' disciples were not following the elaborate ritual of the Jews in ceremonially washing their hands (the issue is Pharisaical "holiness," not personal hygiene), they were criticized before Jesus by the religious leaders (Matthew 15). But Jesus responds to their condemning question with an even stronger one of His own: "Why do *you* break the command of God for the sake of your tradition?" (15:3, emphasis added). Jesus goes on in the passage to show how their unbiblical traditions caused these ultrareligious critics to dishonor their parents (15:4-6), to nullify the Word of God (15:6), to live hypocritical lives (15:7) and to engage in what God considers worthless worship (15:8-9). These are terribly high prices to pay for perpetuating human traditions!

Real Life Says . . .

The world around us doesn't particularly care about our rituals or practices. We Christians may make the equally serious mistakes of either caring too much or caring too little about our traditions. If we care too much, we may be unwilling to look for new ways to communicate God's unchanging truth. We may become slaves to "how we have always done it" instead of eager followers of the God who gives us freedom to change our methods—and our rituals—as long as we are faithful to His Word.

The other error we may commit is caring too little about our traditions. In our "me first" culture, we must ask what impact our practices will have on both the present and future generations. One writer has said that nothing is more deadly in a church than the attitude which has been expressed as, "Come weal or woe; our status is quo!" Living only for ourselves with little thought for the traditions we are developing may be precisely the status quo to be resisted!

But Lord . . .

Father, there is enough rebel in me that I want to overthrow all traditions and start from scratch. Forgive my arrogance and my failure to appreciate those who have gone before me. There is also, Father, enough Pharisee in me that I want to rebuke any who challenge the traditions which I cherish. Please continue the process of giving me both biblical freedom and form as I worship with others. In Jesus' name, Amen.

To Ponder . . .

If you do everything the way everybody has always done it—then you're blind. If you do nothing the way people have always done it—then you're a fool. (Anonymous)

Orthodox, but Ossified!

Believing the right things should lead our hearts into a deeper love relationship with our God.

A real Christian is an odd number, anyway. He feels supreme love for One whom he has never seen; talks familiarly every day to Someone he cannot see; expects to go to heaven on the virtue of Another; empties himself in order to be full; admits he is wrong so he can be declared right; goes down in order to get up; is strongest when he is weakest; richest when he is poorest and happiest when he feels the worst. He dies so he can live; forsakes in order to have; gives away so he can keep; sees the invisible; hears the inaudible; and knows that which passeth knowledge.

(A.W. Tozer)

The way our heart is hardened is by sticking to our convictions instead of to Christ.

(Oswald Chambers)

I know your deeds, your hard work and your perseverance. I know that you cannot tolerate wicked men, that you have tested those who claim to be apostles but are not, and have found them false. You have persevered and have endured hardships for my name, and have not grown weary.

Yet I hold this against you: You have forsaken your first love.

(Revelation 2:2-4)

The Knowledge Nugget

As we have seen, orthodoxy, or right belief, should lead to a joy in the truths of God which manifests itself in an obedience to the Word of God. But, as is so eloquently illustrated by that wayward missionary Jonah (see Day 12), it is quite possible to have correct beliefs without correct behavior.

God asks an extremely personal question in Jeremiah: "Who is he who will devote himself to be close to me?" (Jeremiah 30:21). The book of Revelation shows us that one can have one's beliefs right, have great behavior, but still have a cold heart toward God Himself. God commends the church in Ephesus for several things: "I know your deeds, your hard work and your perseverance. I know that you cannot tolerate wicked men, that you have tested those who claim to be apostles but are not, and have found them false. You have persevered and have endured hardships for my name, and have not grown weary" (Revelation 2:2-3). Hard work, perseverance and the application of theological tests to false teachers are all admirable qualities.

But the Ephesian church is criticized by God for one simple but profound oversight: "You have forsaken your first love" (verse 4). What does it mean to forsake one's first love? Again, God gives the answer through the Old Testament prophet Jeremiah: "My people have committed two sins: They have forsaken me, the spring of living water, and have dug their own cisterns, broken cisterns that cannot hold water" (Jeremiah 2:13).

Our hearts can become hard to the Lord Himself. I heard about one woman who complained to another about her ex-boyfriend: "He wouldn't dare eat his heart out," she said. "He'd break his teeth on it."

When we begin to think that God is more interested in our work *for* Him than our walk *with* Him, or that what we believe *about* Him is more important than our relationship *to* Him, or that He cares more about the *information* we possess than about our *intimacy* with Him, we are in grave danger of losing our first love.

Real Life Says . . .

The world around us is shocked when Christians say that they have a "personal relationship with the God of the Bible." But what counts most in life is not this world's opinion, but the true God's evaluation of us.

To say that one can be orthodox, but *ossified*, is to say that one's heart can become hardened to God Himself. Ossification is the abnormal hardening of soft tissue into a bonelike material. Like the church in Ephesus, each Christian can allow his relationship with God to stop growing, to ossify. And that not only hurts us; it breaks the heart of God.

But Lord . . .

Father, help me to realize that You want it all: my mind, strength, will and heart. Please keep my heart from ossifying, from thinking that having right thoughts of You automatically means growing in my love for You. In Jesus' name, Amen.

To Ponder . . .

We must be careful lest we allow our work for God to squeeze out His work in us. (Bill Hybels)

Today's Focus

To grow deeper in the Christian life we must study the deeper doctrines of the Word of God, refusing to remain infants in our understanding.

Frank Tyger has defined "maturity" as "acting your age instead of your urge."

A popular book of several years ago was entitled: *All I Really Need to Know I Learned in Kindergarten*. Does the Bible agree with that statement?

We have much to say . . . but it is hard to explain because you are slow to learn. In fact, though by this time you ought to be teachers, you need someone to teach you the elementary truths of God's word all over again. You need milk, not solid food! Anyone who lives on milk, being still an infant, is not acquainted with the teaching about righteousness. But solid food is for the mature, who by constant use have trained themselves to distinguish good from evil.

(Hebrews 5:11-14)

The Knowledge Nugget

The excellent Bible teacher Ray Stedman once said in a sermon on Romans 5, "Wherever the Christian church is weak (and it is weak in many places), and wherever Christians are weak individually, it's always because they have never graduated into the high school of the Holy Spirit—they are still babes in Christ, no matter how long they have been Christians." If we look at the Christian life as a kind of educational progression, some believers might be in that "high school of the Holy Spirit," some have not yet made it out of elementary school, and perhaps many are stuck in nursery school!

As we saw in our devotional on Day 3 ("Who Needs Theology?"), the writer to the Hebrews minces no words when he criticizes them for their failure to progress in doctrinal depth. "In fact," he says, "some of you should be teachers, but you are in need of remedial summer school in the basics of the faith!" (see Hebrews 5:12). Their "learning disabilities" included the fact that they were "slow to learn" (5:11), presumably because they chose to stay where they were.

The writer of Hebrews moves to a second image to illustrate the need to mature in the truths of God. He contrasts one who lives on milk with one who is able to take in solid food or meat (5:13-14). Contrary to the old advertising slogan, "Milk does a body good!" the writer indicates that a strict milk diet makes a milquetoast Christian. (If you're like me, you had to look up the term "milquetoast." It originally meant a bland dish of hot buttered toast in warm milk [yuk!], but now means a frail person.) That's not the kind of believer God wants to produce. We are not meant to be spiritual vegetarians; we need to sink our teeth deep into the meat of the Word if we are going to be strong in this confused and starving world.

Real Life Says . . .

Many in this world believe that we Christians are an odd lot. We would lay down our lives for a Savior we have never seen, we regularly talk to a God who has not appeared to us and we studiously try to align our lives with an ancient book which was originally written in

Hebrew, Aramaic and Greek! And when our beliefs or our moral values are attacked, some of us collapse into conformity.

The book of Hebrews gives us the answer to a spineless, wishy-washy spiritual life, and the answer is a change in diet! We must move from the milk of the Word to the meat of the Word, and in so doing, we will be "trained . . . to distinguish good from evil" (5:14).

My wife filled the cat's food dish, but the cat still seemed to be hungry. When I checked, I discovered she had put kitty litter instead of cat food in the dish—hardly a nourishing meal! (I probably would have made the same mistake; after all, with kitty litter named "Cat's Choice," it sounded like a gourmet feast!) Some of our choices for spiritual nourishment can be just as mistaken. We need to remember that *God's* choice for us is the filet mignon of His Word!

But Lord . . .

Father, I praise You for the provision in Your Word of both milk and meat. Help me to become a well-fed teacher of Your truth by the life I lead in Christ. In Jesus' name, Amen.

To Ponder . . .

How nutritious is your spiritual diet?

Adorning the Doctrine

It is difficult to argue with a changed life. And if we believe the doctrines of the Bible, our lives should show positive changes.

Every Bible should be bound by shoe leather.

(D.L. Moody)

So live your life today that your pastor won't have to lie about you at your funeral.

(Anonymous)

Teach slaves to be subject to their masters in everything, to try to please them, not to talk back to them, and not to steal from them, but to show that they can be fully trusted, so that in every way they will make the teaching about God our Savior attractive.

(Titus 2:9-10)

The Knowledge Nugget

Paderewski, the Polish pianist, composer and statesman, was once conducting a symphony. He became quite agitated and began to yell at the orchestra. He stepped off the podium, then came back and apologized to the orchestra, commenting, "The problem is Beethoven and I know how to play the music, and you keep getting in the way!"

Sometimes we can "get in the way" of the wonderful truths of God's Word because of our poor conduct. We make God look bad before others, especially when we fail to practice what we preach.

The Apostle Paul gives his spiritual son Titus some critical advice about living out the Christian faith, with specific instructions for various groups in the church. Clear directions are spelled out by Paul for elders (1:5-9), for those older in the faith (2:1-2), for the mature women (2:3), for the younger women with families (2:4-5) and for the young men (2:6-8). The last group Paul addresses are the *slaves* in Titus' congregation!

The Bible does not condone slavery; in fact, Paul himself comes to the conclusion that "there is neither . . . slave nor free . . . for you are all one in Christ Jesus" (Galatians 3:28). One would think, therefore, that Paul would say something like, "Tell the slaves that they are free! And rebuke those who have such control over other men's lives!" But that's not what he does. As important as physical freedom is, Paul has a larger agenda.

He advises the slaves under Titus' spiritual care to model godly behavior "so that in every way they will make the teaching about God our Savior attractive" (Titus 2:10). If we may expand that advice given to slaves to all believers in Christ, has it ever crossed your mind that we make God's truths attractive—or repulsive—by our conduct?

Real Life Says . . .

Many today seem to believe that if a Christian does not perfectly model what he says he believes, his belief must be ridiculous. Others take the opposite view and divorce conduct from concept. The value of a belief, they suggest, is not dependent on whether or not *anyone* practices it! I'm not sure, however, that many are attracted to a belief which provides no visible demonstration of its value.

The believer in Jesus Christ is to model the truth of God. That means we have to readily admit when our belief and behavior fail to match! Someone has wisely said, "The greatest thing about being a Christian is that I no longer have to defend my own goodness." But the Christian is under obligation to "flesh out" what biblical Christianity really teaches.

An athlete may get away with stepping out of bounds or committing a personal foul in a practice game where no score is kept. But in a championship game, it's a different story. When we fail to "make the teaching about God our Savior attractive," we can count on the fact that those who observe our lives are keeping score!

But Lord . . .

Father, remind me that I am to embody Your truth by the power of Your Holy Spirit. Forgive me when I cost You "votes." Help me to be quick to acknowledge my own failings before others, so they don't blame You for my poor conduct. In Jesus' name, Amen.

To Ponder . . .

"Words, words, words, I'm sick of words. Sing me no song, read me no rhyme, don't waste my time. Show me." (*My Fair Lady*)

Doubt, Misbelief or Unbelief?

Doubt need not necessarily lead to unbelief, but can be a stimulus to faith in God's truth.

Doubt is probably a permanent feature of the Christian life. It's like some kind of spiritual growing pain. Sometimes, it recedes into the background; at other times it comes to the fore, making its presence felt with a vengeance.

(Alister McGrath)

I have found that petty disappointments tend to accumulate over time, undermining my faith with a lava flow of doubt.

(Philip Yancey)

Then [Jesus] said to Thomas, "Put your finger here; see my hands. Reach out your hand and put it into my side. Stop doubting and believe."

(John 20:27)

The Knowledge Nugget

A number of years ago there was a television comedy entitled "Perfect Strangers." Larry and his cousin Balki were always getting into trouble. On one show, Balki, who always seemed to struggle with how to say something in his new language of English, had to admit that he was greatly mistaken about a situation. He said, "Larry, I'm so sorry. I know now that I was *misconceived*!"

Is it not the case that our *ideas* are often misconceived? We find ourselves sometimes believing what we should not believe (I call this "misbelief") and at other times not believing what we should believe (this would be "unbelief"). And frequently we struggle in that twilight zone between genuine faith and real unbelief, becoming dominated by *doubt*.

One of my favorite characters in Scripture has unfortunately been misnamed. I am speaking of "Doubting Thomas." This is the disciple in John 20 who refused to believe that Jesus had risen from the dead and needed to be convinced by a personal resurrection appearance of the Lord Himself.

In his book *In Two Minds*, Os Guinness says that to believe is to be "in one mind" about accepting something as true; to disbelieve is to be "in one mind" about rejecting it. To doubt is to waver between the two, to believe and disbelieve at once and so be "in two minds." When we look at "Doubting Thomas" in John 20, we see that he was not bound by doubt, but by *adamant unbelief*. To the disciples who were proclaiming that Christ had risen, he declared, "Unless I see the nail marks in his hands and put my finger where the nails were, and put my hand into his side, I will not believe it" (20:25). Notice that Thomas does not simply demand a personal resurrection appearance of the Lord; he insists on a virtual *autopsy*. (By the way, the word "autopsy" comes from two words: one meaning "self" and the other meaning "to see"!) Thomas may have been exaggerating when he insisted on putting his finger where the nails were and his hand into Christ's side, but he is clearly saying, "*I will by no means believe* He has risen from the dead" (the emphasis of the Greek words). I think we should rename him "Adamantly Unbelieving Thomas."

Thomas' demand is met by the Lord, and this unbelieving disciple falls at the risen Lord's feet, declaring Jesus to be "My Lord and my

God!" (20:28). He is rebuked by Jesus—not for demanding evidence for the resurrection—but for insisting on more evidence than he needed (20:29).

Real Life Says . . .

A revolution has taken place in our culture. For many people, belief and facts do not need to have anything to do with one another. Misbelief is considered an "alternative viewpoint." Unbelief is admired by many as "independent thinking." And doubt seems to be the highest virtue of some in academic circles. Christian theology teaches that God has made His truth clear in the Bible. And there are good reasons to respond to God's truth by belief rather than unbelief or doubt. Doubt could be a positive step toward genuine belief, if the evidence is examined and one responds to the truth.

But Lord . . .

Lord, I really want to affirm Your truth. Forgive me when I choose to believe myself or my culture instead of You! Please continue Your work in me in making me a person of faith. In Jesus' name, Amen.

To Ponder . . .

"If you would be a real seeker after truth, it is necessary that at least once in your life you doubt, as far as possible, all things," said Descartes. Is this Christian advice?

Plundering the Egyptians

To "plunder the Egyptians" means to use whatever resources are available (even from non-Christian thinkers) to assist the teaching of biblical truth.

A Roman Catholic priest was quite upset at Erasmus' Greek New Testament. England's King Henry VIII asked the priest, "Have you *read* Erasmus?"

"No, sire," said the priest.

"Then away from me," the king replied. "You are a blockhead!"

"For in him we live and move and have our being." As some of your own poets have said, "We are his offspring."

(Acts 17:28)

Even one of their own prophets has said, "Cretans are always liars, evil brutes, lazy gluttons." This testimony is true. Therefore, rebuke them sharply, so that they will be sound in the faith and will pay no attention to Jewish myths or to the commands of those who reject the truth.

(Titus 1:12-14)

The Knowledge Nugget

When Israel was rescued from Egypt, we read that "the Israelites did as Moses instructed and asked the Egyptians for articles of silver and gold and for clothing. The LORD had made the Egyptians favorably disposed toward the people, and they gave them what they asked for; *so they plundered the Egyptians*" (Exodus 12:35-36, emphasis added).

There are many Christians who think that the only book they should ever read is the Bible. And, of course, the Word of God must not only be our foundation for what we believe, but also our filter to separate out the things we should not believe. But the Apostle Paul gives evidence that he read books other than the Old Testament (the New Testament had not yet been completed). In fact, he quotes from well-known Greek poets and dramatists in Acts 17:28 and Titus 1:12-14. He uses truth which he finds in nonbiblical sources to relate to and attempts to persuade his non-Christian audience. This is what we mean by "plundering the Egyptians." Because all people are made in the image of God, even the most anti-Christian writer will occasionally say something true!

To be sure, the frequent and indiscriminate reading of authors who reject the truths of the Bible has its dangers. The story is told of a man in India who was searching for a particular book in a library. He felt a pain in his finger like the prick of a pin. He took little notice of it but soon his arm began to swell. In a short time he was dead. A small but deadly serpent was found among the books. The writer who tells the story warns us, "There are many who receive in a book a bad wound that may seem slight, but proves fatal to the soul. Be careful what you read." But we should not overreact.

The Christian who is growing deep in the things of God will make careful use of material outside the Bible so that he can communicate to those not yet in the family of God. I understand that several centuries ago 700,000 valuable Alexandrian documents were destroyed by the followers of Islam. They explained their action by saying, "Either these books conform to the Koran or they do not. If they do, they are not needed. If they do not, they are harmful. Therefore, let them be destroyed." That should not be the attitude of the believer in Christ!

Real Life Says . . .

Our surrounding culture does not see any one book as finally authoritative. The idea that the Bible is the thoroughly trustworthy communication of the true God seems ludicrous to many, so the idea of "plundering the Egyptians" seems silly at best or arrogant at worst. But the believer in Jesus Christ acknowledges the authority of the Word of God and seeks to grow in its truths. At the same time, the serious disciple should read material outside of the Bible in order to learn what the nonbeliever thinks and how to communicate the gospel in terms which can be understood.

But Lord . . .

Father, help me to recognize that in Christ I have the freedom to read anything that helps me to share my faith in You. Thank You that all human beings are made in Your image, and no one can escape that fact! Give me wisdom to sort out truth from error. In Jesus' name, Amen.

To Ponder . . .

Aleksandr Solzhenitsyn quoted a Russian proverb as he received the Nobel prize for literature: "One word of truth outweighs the whole world."

How Are Your Studies Coming?

To grow in the truths of God involves dedicating oneself to studying His Word and everything which helps one's advancement in sound doctrine.

Many people think that research is a supernatural gift of the gods. It is simply an idea from a troubled mind, an inspiration followed by infinitely painstaking work and perspiration.

(Sir Frederick Banting)

Spare no pains to study Scripture in order to expound it accurately and meaningfully. This calls for a greater measure of integrity than we often display. If the Bible is God's Word written, we must pray over it and pore over it until it yields its message. We have no liberty to falsify the Word of God, twisting it to suit our prejudice or to conceal our laziness.

(John R.W. Stott)

Study to shew thyself approved unto God, a workman that needeth not to be ashamed, rightly dividing the word of truth.

(2 Timothy 2:15, KJV)

The Knowledge Nugget

Every year in Yellowstone National Park, after tourist season is over and the snow falls, dozens of bears die by the side of the road. Park rangers say that the bears starve to death, waiting for handouts from the tourists. They become so dependent on humans for their food that their natural instinct to forage becomes short-circuited.

What a picture that story is of many Christians! We believers often suffer from the habit of letting others do our biblical study and thinking for us. *They* invest the time and energy in pursuing the truths of God, as *we* wait to be spoon-fed.

In Second Timothy 2:15, Paul admonishes this young leader to take responsibility for his own spiritual growth. I prefer the King James translation of that verse: "Study to shew thyself approved unto God, a workman that needeth not to be ashamed, rightly dividing the word of truth." The word "study" is a term which means to be diligent. The follower of Jesus Christ is to be diligent in studying the Word of God so that he will not need to be ashamed, but will be able to correctly interpret ("divide") the Bible.

Real Life Says . . .

Some in our culture suggest that we must have religious experts do our thinking for us. Others put more emphasis on individual experiences than on the careful study of the Bible. I remember an adult Sunday school teacher who had us do a simple observation exercise in a chapter of John's Gospel. One of the women chose not to do the exercise, preferring to share "from her heart" what she thought the passage was saying!

But Christians must recognize that God's truth does not come naturally to us. Diligent study must be applied for that truth to become ours. As we saw in our devotional on church history (Day 11), this is not to suggest that we study the Bible in isolation from the Spirit's work in the lives of other believers.

We do new believers no favor when we suggest that all they have to do to grow in the truths of God is to show up in the pew a couple of times a week and get it by osmosis. Osmosis, as you may know, refers to "any gradual, often unconscious, process of assimilation or absorption that resembles the diffusion of fluid through a semipermeable membrane until there is an equal concentration of fluid on either side of the membrane."

What?!?

In layman's terms, we act in the church as if simply *being there* is enough to grow us up in the faith. And that simply is not true. Growing deep in the things of God does not happen by osmosis!

But Lord . . .

Father, I have to confess that sometimes I am simply flat-out lazy. Thank You for Your truth that is there for me to discover for myself. Guide me as I live out my life as a student of Your Word. In Jesus' name, Amen.

To Ponder . . .

Matthew Poole, a Puritan writer, once admonished some young preachers, "Don't be so arrogant as to think that you can stand and teach the Word of God without study, study, study!"

What's So Liberal about Liberal Theology?

There are individuals who claim to love Jesus, but who do not accept the inspiration of the Bible, the need for a Redeemer or the deity of Christ. Liberal theology denies the fundamental truths of the Christian faith and is anything but "liberal."

A God without wrath brought men without sin into a kingdom without judgment through the ministrations of a Christ without a Cross.

(H. Richard Neibuhr)

Schleiermacher [a famous liberal theologian] told his readers that the days of fairy tales are over and we need not worry our heads about the supernatural in Christianity.

(Bernard Ramm)

Shun profane and vain babblings; for they will increase unto more ungodliness. And their word will eat as doth a canker: of whom is Hymenaeus and Philetus; who concerning the truth have erred, saying that the resurrection is past already; and overthrow the faith of some.

(2 Timothy 2:16-18, KJV)

The Knowledge Nugget

The term "liberal" originally meant to be generous or bountiful, coming from a Latin word meaning freedom. But liberal theology is neither generous nor bountiful, nor does it bestow freedom. This theological orientation *takes away* the fundamentals of the Christian faith, replacing such doctrines as the trustworthiness of the Bible, the deity of Christ and the need for forgiveness by a righteous God, with human ideas of religious evolution, the divinity of all people and an emphasis on God's "love" which implies that no one will ever be judged.

The liberal theologian Nels F.S. Ferré is famous for his statement that "heaven can only be heaven when it has emptied hell!" He referred to the Bible as a "first-century museum" and spent his life arguing that all without exception will be saved, a heresy known as universalism.

Liberal theology dominates the departments of religion in many universities and seminaries. Whether we are speaking of individuals like Charles Templeton, a former coevangelist with Billy Graham who has now renounced his belief in God (see his book *Farewell to God*), or the Episcopal priest John Spong who wants to retain the love of God without the atoning work of Christ (see his evangelical-bashing book *Rescuing the Bible from Fundamentalism*), liberal theologians mock doctrines like everlasting punishment, the inerrancy of Scripture, the uniqueness of Christ, etc.

Adolf Harnack, a famous German church historian, was criticized by a contemporary (Stocker) for his liberalism. He said that Harnack had

> no respect for history, no honor for the confessions, no regard for the Church and community. Hypotheses, quite often giddy hypotheses . . . are given greater reality than the foundation beliefs of the Church. . . . The confession, biblical authority, and finally the historicity and the personality of Christ himself are thrown into the witches' kettle of frothy criticism.

Real Life Says . . .

Liberals often appear as the intellectual heroes to an unbelieving world. They question—and, at times, ridicule—the precious doctrines of the biblical faith. When *they* are criticized by the church, the church is accused of being narrow-minded, on a witch-hunt, or simply uncharitable.

When the Apostle Paul spoke about theological error in Second Timothy 2, he minced no words. Calling such teachings "profane and vain babblings," he warned that false doctrine will lead to false living ("ungodliness"). And Paul was not reluctant to name names! We see in other passages that Paul spoke about those who deserted him: "You know that everyone in the province of Asia has deserted me, including Phygelus and Hermogenes" (2 Timothy 1:15). He also spoke of those who have made spiritual shipwreck of their faith (naming this same Hymenaeus): "Some have rejected [faith and a good conscience]. . . . Among them are Hymenaeus and Alexander, whom I have handed over to Satan to be taught not to blaspheme" (1 Timothy 1:19-20). He also spoke of "Demas, [who] because he loved this world, has deserted me and has gone to Thessalonica" (2 Timothy 4:10). "Alexander the metalworker," says Paul, "did me a great deal of harm. The Lord will repay him for what he has done" (4:14).

In a passage mentioned earlier, Paul charged Hymenaeus and Philetus with teaching a wrong view of the resurrection. Their perspective was hardly innocent. In the language of the King James Bible, it "eat[s] as doth a canker" (cancer) (2:17, KJV) and overthrows the faith of some of the believers. There is nothing benign about false teaching!

But Lord . . .

Father, let me be liberal in Your truth! And give me diligence in defending the doctrines of Your Word. In Jesus' name, Amen.

To Ponder . . .

We belong to a God who gives *liberally* (James 1:5, KJV), but He does not give beliefs which run counter to His Word!

Slip Slidin' Away

When Christians wander from the truths of the Word of God, there may be many reasons. The process of restoration involves the love of God's people (the church) and a definite discipleship which emphasizes the ignored or rejected doctrines.

If you examined a hundred people who had lost their faith in Christianity, I wonder how many of them would turn out to have been reasoned out of it by honest argument? Do not most people simply drift away?

(C.S. Lewis)

The explorer Daniel Boone was once asked if he ever got lost. "No," he said, "but I was a mite bewildered for three days once."

For the love of money is a root of all kinds of evil. Some people, eager for money, have wandered from the faith and pierced themselves with many griefs. . . .

Timothy, guard what has been entrusted to your care. Turn away from godless chatter and the opposing ideas of what is falsely called knowledge, which some have professed and in so doing have wandered from the faith.

(1 Timothy 6:10, 20-21)

The Knowledge Nugget

Many years ago a little boy and his twin sister became lost in a small community outside Boston. After they were missing for several hours, the police were called and a search party was organized. Meanwhile, the little boy and girl both showed up when they heard the commotion as the search party got organized. They asked what was going on and were told that a little boy and girl had been lost. For the next two hours they helped search for themselves!

In spiritual matters Christians aren't good at searching for themselves. That's why we need the church. Its "search and rescue" division enlists all believers in recovering those who wander away.

A surprisingly large amount of attention is devoted in the New Testament to this problem of spiritual straying (see 2 Timothy 2:17 and James 5:19-20). Some strayers become possessed by possessions and begin a self-destructive journey away from God. Paul wrote to Timothy, "For the love of money is a root of all kinds of evil. Some people, eager for money, have wandered from the faith and pierced themselves with many griefs" (1 Timothy 6:10). Contrary to popular opinion, this verse does not say that money is the root of all evil, but that the *love of money* is *a root* of all kinds of evil.

Note that Paul says there are dire consequences for those who wander from the faith. They pierce "themselves with many griefs." I understand that in World War II some Japanese soldiers committed a particular form of suicide when they knew they would be captured by Allied troops. Originally used only by the upper classes, this ritual suicide by disembowelment was called *hara-kiri*. In a sense, Paul is saying that spiritual strayers commit spiritual hara-kiri when they depart from God's truth.

Real Life Says . . .

One should not be surprised that the concept of spiritual straying makes little sense in a world which denies absolute truth. If there is no definite path to travel in life, then all of one's existence is wandering around, moving from one belief to another in a quest for meaning.

But the Apostle Paul admonishes Timothy to "guard what has been entrusted to your care. Turn away from godless chatter and the opposing ideas of what is falsely called knowledge, which some have professed and in so doing have wandered from the faith" (6:20-21). The Christian response to spiritual straying is threefold: we are to guard the truth of God, to turn away from godless chatter and to intervene in the lives of those who wander away.

Sir Thomas Beecham was having some difficulties conducting a choral group in the magnificent music of Handel's *Messiah*. "Ladies and gentlemen," he chided. "If you will make a point of singing 'All we like sheep have gone astray,' with a little less satisfaction, we'll meet the aesthetical as well as the theological requirements."

But Lord . . .

Father, I am "prone to wander" from Your truth. Bind my wandering heart to Thee. Give me Your love for those who stray—and keep me on Your true path. In Jesus' name, Amen.

To Ponder . . .

"My brothers, if one of you should wander from the truth and someone should bring him back, remember this: Whoever turns a sinner from the error of his way will save him from death and cover over a multitude of sins." (James 5:19-20)

From Amusement to Amazement

Today's Focus

Growing in the doctrines of the Christian faith will take our attention off ourselves and our own entertainment and focus our hearts on God and His truths.

If and when American civilization collapses, historians of a future date can look back and sneer, "They entertained themselves to death."

(Anonymous)

If you would rule the world quietly, you must keep it amused.

(Ralph Waldo Emerson)

Oh, the depth of the riches of the
    wisdom and knowledge of God!
  How unsearchable his judgments,
  and his paths beyond tracing out!
"Who has known the mind of the Lord?
  Or who has been his counselor?"
"Who has ever given to God,
  that God should repay him?"
For from him and through him and to
    him are all things.
To him be the glory forever! Amen.

(Romans 11:33-36)

The Knowledge Nugget

When a believer in Jesus Christ takes responsibility for his own spiritual growth, refusing to blame others for any lack of progress in the Christian faith (remember Day 14, "Water Your Faith!"), that Christian has begun a glorious journey! That journey involves serious study by the disciple, as we saw in the devotional for Day 25, "How Are Your Studies Coming?"

One of the greatest roadblocks to that glorious journey in the truths of God is not persecution or poverty, but what appears to be this country's gross national product: entertainment. Many feel they are "owed" entertainment, especially on their free time. It seems that many have bought into the philosophy expressed in a recent hair color commercial: "I'm worth it!"

Real Life Says . . .

Our Western culture suggests that every human being is entitled to "life, liberty and the pursuit of happiness." Many major in pursuing the pleasures of this world and minor in pursuing the God "at [whose] right hand there are pleasures for evermore" (Psalm 16:11, KJV). They suffer from longings that are too meager, aspirations that are earthbound and transient. They have been taken hostage by the insatiable quest for everything but God.

Much the same could be said about many a Christian. Why are more believers not earnestly seeking to grow deep in doctrine? There may be many reasons, but one primary reason was suggested by A.W. Tozer long ago. He wrote in his monumental work, *The Pursuit of God*,

> Everything is made to center upon the initial act of "accepting" Christ (a term, incidentally, which is not found in the Bible) and we are not expected thereafter to crave any further revelation of God to our souls. We have been snared in the coils of a spurious logic which insists that if we have found Him we need no more seek Him.

Would it not be a fair definition of salvation to say that when an individual is soundly converted, he moves from the category of *amusement* to the category of *amazement*? The term "amusement," by the way, literally means "not to think"! God wakes us up by His grace and begins the process in us of helping us to think—to think about Him, about His plan for our lives and about His truths, which we desperately need.

In today's passage (Romans 11:33-36), Paul, overwhelmed with the magnificence of knowing the Lord, rebukes all shallow living of lazy saints: "Oh, the depth of the riches of the wisdom and knowledge of God!" He follows this first exclamation with two others: "How unsearchable his judgments, and his paths beyond tracing out!" His words appear intended to inspire us to wonder and seek God further, rather than to give up the quest to know God better.

He follows his three exclamations with three profound questions: "Who has known the mind of the Lord? Or who has been his counselor? Who has ever given to God, that God should repay him?" The first two questions are from Isaiah 40; the third from Job 41. Paul's point was the greatness and uniqueness of God. He is dependent on no one. And He is no one's debtor!

Such contemplation of God should move us from amusement to amazement. We should say with the Apostle Paul: "For from him and through him and to him are all things. To him be the glory forever! Amen" (Romans 11:36).

But Lord . . .

Father, help me to learn to think! And to stand amazed in Your presence! In Jesus' name, Amen.

To Ponder . . .

The real "muse" is someone who thinks the thoughts of God as found in His Word!

Very Superstitious!

Biblical faith is not superstition. Biblical faith—that is, believing what God says is true—rests upon the character of God, and not upon concepts of luck, fate or chance.

Superstition is a pernicious emperor who rules in the world throughout the ages and whose rule the people of the world are glad to accept.

(Martin Luther)

We would be a lot safer if the government would take its money out of science and put it into astrology and the reading of palms. Only in superstition is there hope. If you want to become a friend of civilization, then become an enemy of the truth and a fanatic for harmless balderdash.

(Kurt Vonnegut Jr.)

We did not follow cleverly invented stories when we told you about the power and coming of our Lord Jesus Christ, but we were eyewitnesses of his majesty.

(2 Peter 1:16)

The Knowledge Nugget

There is an American proverb that says, "It is bad luck to fall out of a thirteenth story window on a Friday." Someone has defined superstition as "any belief, practice or rite unreasoningly upheld by faith in magic, chance or dogma." Another definition simply says that super-stition is "idolatry."

Wade Boggs, famous Yankee baseball player and five-time winner of the American League batting title, believes he hits better after hav-ing a meal of chicken. Not surprisingly Boggs has eaten chicken every day for the last twenty years. He has even published his own cook-book of his favorite chicken recipes! Superstitions are quite common among professional athletes.

They are also common among the general population. People cross their fingers, knock on wood, go out of their way to avoid a black cat or refuse to walk under a ladder. Where do these ideas come from? The answer may surprise you. Scholars tell us, for example, that a ladder leaning against a wall forms a triangle, the symbol of the Trinity and of the mystic number three. Many thought that to walk through the trian-gle would be to defy the Trinity and risk divine wrath. (I'm not supersti-tious, but I think not walking under a ladder is a good idea—there might be a bucket of paint or a hammer up there, waiting for a target!)

The term "superstition" occurs only once in the Bible. The context is the Apostle Paul's being questioned before King Agrippa. We read that the Jews "had certain questions against [Paul] of their own *super-stition*, and of one Jesus, which was dead, whom Paul affirmed to be alive" (Acts 25:19, KJV). This would not be the last occasion in which biblical belief would be called "superstition."

Real Life Says . . .

Many in our culture see little difference between biblical faith and superstition. The late Carl Sagan once said, "It is far better to grasp the universe as it really is than to persist in delusion, however satisfy-ing and reassuring." Emerson declared that "As men's prayers are a disease of the will, so are their creeds a disease of the intellect."

Does the Christian suffer from delusion, from a disease of the intellect? The Apostle Peter insists that we have not followed "cleverly invented stories" in choosing to believe in Jesus Christ. Growing in the doctrines of the Bible is not superstition, for there are good and sufficient reasons for accepting the Bible's material.

In his song "Superstition," Stevie Wonder says several common beliefs keep us in a "daydream." His chorus gives us both truth and error: "When you believe in things that you don't understand, Then you suffer, Superstition ain't the way." Every day, all human beings "believe" in things they don't understand. I "believe" my car will start, although I don't completely understand how it works. But superstition is not the same as belief. If Christian belief is grounded in the character of the living God, then it is not superstition. And what one *doesn't believe* will cause one to suffer!

But Lord . . .

Lord, I must admit that sometimes my faith seems like superstition. When I think that carrying a Bible will protect me from harm, or having my quiet time will guarantee me a good day, or attending church will keep my children out of trouble, I have ventured out of biblical faith into superstitious living. Help me to believe Your truth and to show a watching world that faith in Christ is not magic, delusion or intellectual suicide. In Jesus' name, Amen.

To Ponder . . .

When a person does not believe God, all that's left is superstition!

Theology Is Not Boring!

If theology is the engagement of one's total being in the truths of God, then there is no room for boredom!

Life's real enemy is not pain, not even death; life's enemy is boredom.

(Walter Burghardt)

It is not true at all that dogma is "hopelessly irrelevant" to the life and thought of the average man. What is true is that ministers . . . often assert that it is, present it for consideration as though it were, and, in fact, by their faulty exposition of it make it so.

(Dorothy Sayers)

I pray that out of his glorious riches he may strengthen you with power through his Spirit in your inner being, so that Christ may dwell in your hearts through faith. And I pray that you, being rooted and established in love, may have power, together with all the saints, to grasp how wide and long and high and deep is the love of Christ, and to know this love that surpasses knowledge—that you may be filled to the measure of all the fullness of God.

(Ephesians 3:16-19)

The Knowledge Nugget

A mother tells about raising her teenage son. She says that someone told her that she would get some respect from him if she stressed the fact that she had given him birth. During one argument she said, "Remember, son, I bore you."

"Yes, Mom," he shot back, "sometimes you do!"

The widely held view that theology, the study of God and the things of God, is boring needs to be refuted. As I often tell my seminary students, "Theology is not boring. *Theologians* may be boring, yes, but not theology!"

The earlier quote by the great English writer Dorothy Sayers says it well. By "dogma" she means the doctrines of the Christian faith. Her criticism is mainly directed to preachers who show little or no enthusiasm for the truths of God. Which reminds me of the pastor who met one of his delinquent members and said, "I haven't seen you in church much lately."

"Well," the church member replied, "you know how it's been. The children have been sick, and then it's rained and rained."

"It's always dry at church," the pastor said.

"It sure is," he agreed. "That's another reason why I haven't been coming."

In an article on boredom, Saul Bellow tells us that

> the brain—whether a worm's, a rat's or a human's—needs something to chew on. At its simplest level, boredom is the brain's pained response to nothingness or to endless repetition. The discomfort of boredom, like the gnawing of an empty stomach, is the brain's way of saying it's hungry. . . . The human mind in a high-tech society, with endless options for distracting, entertaining and narcotizing itself, cannot escape boredom solely by keeping busy. . . . Boredom is a kind of pain caused by unused powers, the pain of

wasted possibilities of the optimum utilization of capacities.

Real Life Says . . .

Our surrounding culture drugs itself against boredom by overindulgence in entertainment (see Day 28, "From Amusement to Amazement"), by addiction to technology or by serial relationships. The cure for boredom is truth—God's truth!

When we Christians are only spoon-fed, we should not be surprised that boredom results. Paul's packed paragraph to the Ephesian believers (3:16-19) holds several keys to cure boredom: He emphasizes that Christian strength comes out of God's "glorious riches." Power for living the Christian life comes from being "rooted and established" in God's love. And every believer is to pursue the endless quest of knowing the love "that surpasses knowledge." The ultimate goal, Paul says, is that the believer "may be filled to the measure of all the fullness of God." If theology is understood to be the engagement of one's heart, mind and will in the truths of God, then life is too short for boredom!

But Lord . . .

Father, thank You for the endless excitement that comes from knowing You. Guide me in my adventure of growing in Your truths. In Jesus' name, Amen.

To Ponder . . .

The cure for boredom is curiosity. There is no cure for curiosity. (Ellen Parr)

Section Two:

The Absolute Need
for an Absolute Authority

A Brief Preview

"One man's opinion is as good as another's," suggests our world. How misguided such an attitude is!

The second section of this volume asks the fundamental question of religious authority. What we believe should not ultimately be determined by personal experience, human reason or even church tradition. The believer in Jesus Christ is to be a life-long student of the Word of God, the Bible.

The Scriptures are the most relevant book in human history, providing true riches, strength for serving Christ and a firm foundation to keep the Christian steady in the storms of life. Only a full commitment to the inerrancy and authority of the Bible will lead the believer in Jesus Christ on to maturity. Such an understanding of the Word of God will make the Christian dangerous—in a good sense—and free to live boldly like the Savior in this truth-starved world.

Where Did You Get That Idea?

The sources of theology, or of what people believe, are often varied and unrecognized. One of the most fundamental questions to answer concerns this issue of religious authority.

The most important person to listen to is oneself, and our most important task is to develop an ear that can really hear what we are saying.

(Sydney Harris)

I have made a covenant with God that He sends me neither visions, dreams, nor even angels. I am well satisfied with the gift of the Holy Scriptures which give me abundant instruction and all that I need to know both for this life and for that which is to come.

(Martin Luther)

Heaven and earth will pass away, but my words will never pass away.

(Jesus in Matthew 24:35)

The Knowledge Nugget

What people believe is determined by what they consider their religious authority to be. Although many have not consciously asked themselves the question, "*Why* do I believe that?" the deeper question is *what* determines what I (or you) believe.

There are many sources for beliefs in our world. Some consult their daily horoscope (a practice explicitly forbidden by the Bible); Christians often parrot what they have heard from their pastor. Still others claim they believe only those things which have been "proven" by modern science (although some of the most important truths in life cannot fit into a test tube!).

My family and I recently went to a Chinese restaurant. At the end of the meal we engaged in that long-standing tradition of cracking open and reading aloud our fortunes from our respective fortune cookies. Most were innocuous. Mine said, "The next request you make of a loved one will not be denied." I turned to my wife before I read mine out loud and asked, "Will you give me a big kiss right here in this restaurant?" She turned me down—and then I showed her my fortune from my fortune cookie! In the Old Testament, those who claimed to be prophets but whose prophecies did not come true were stoned to death. What should be done with false fortune cookie writers?

I've always dreamed of sneaking into a fortune cookie factory and inserting Bible verses, such as, "It is a dreadful thing to fall into the hands of the living God" (Hebrews 10:31) or "If anyone's name was not found written in the book of life, he was thrown into the lake of fire" (Revelation 20:15). Sayings such as those would cause many to choke on their Moo Goo Gai Pan!

Although there are numerous sources for what people believe, they inevitably boil down to four major ones: experience, reason, church tradition and revelation. We will look at each of these in our next four devotionals. Each of these sources fulfills an important function, but only the Bible, the Word of God, should be our final authority for what we believe and practice.

Real Life Says . . .

Our world gives quite confusing messages. On the one hand, it insists that each person can believe whatever he wants, no matter how bizarre, as long as it does not hurt others or drain the national budget. Such "tolerance" explains the pluralism of our society, an environment which defends *every* belief, no matter how ridiculous. As G.K. Chesterton put it, "When people cease to believe in God, they do not believe in nothing. They believe in anything!"

Our society also communicates the message in no uncertain terms that no one dare be certain or exclusive about his belief system. To profess to have an authority that stands in judgment over all other authorities is audacious at best and downright dangerous at worst, our world believes.

What do Christians do with the absolutely exclusive statement of the Lord Jesus Christ when He says, "Heaven and earth will pass away, but my words will never pass away" (Matthew 24:35)? Whatever is not consistent with His Word is presently under judgment. And we Christians can't (and shouldn't) dodge that reality.

Although there are important functions of experience, reason and church tradition, none of these should be the final authority for what we believe or practice. Only the Word of God, the Bible, has that power!

But, Lord . . .

Father, keep me fixed on Your Word as my final authority in all I believe and practice. In Jesus' name, Amen.

To Ponder . . .

People are experts in hearing what they want to hear, so they can believe what they want to believe, so they can do what they want to do. (Stephen Brown)

And Now, in First Place: Personal Experience!

Our experiences in life, even those that may seem to be supernatural, are to be evaluated by their conformity, or lack of conformity, to the Bible, the Word of God.

Can you imagine if Galileo had been a baby boomer? He would have proved that the universe revolved around *him*.

(Jay Trachman)

One minister reportedly has written in the front flyleaf of his Bible: "I don't care what the Bible says. I've had an experience!"

Evidently some people are throwing you into confusion and are trying to pervert the gospel of Christ. But even if we or an angel from heaven should preach a gospel other than the one we preached to you, let him be eternally condemned! As we have already said, so now I say again: If anybody is preaching to you a gospel other than what you accepted, let him be eternally condemned!

(Galatians 1:7-9)

The Knowledge Nugget

In their search for a religious authority, some people put all their hope in their own experience. It doesn't matter to them what the Bible says, or what Christians teach—their own experience is final and absolute. Syndicated columnist Sydney Harris reflects this attitude in his quote from yesterday's devotional: "The most important person to listen to is oneself, and our most important task is to develop an ear that can really hear what we are saying." I am reminded of the late Erma Bombeck's comment when she said she had just read a book entitled *How to Be Your Own Best Friend*. She said, "The last time I tried to be a friend to myself, I took me to lunch, gained three pounds and have been suspicious of me ever since."

The Apostle Paul emphasizes that any source of information (whether human or angelic) that proclaims a different gospel than the biblical one is to be rejected and condemned. In fact, Paul includes himself as one who could hypothetically preach a false message about Christ: "Even if we or an angel from heaven should preach a gospel other than the one we preached to you, let him be eternally condemned!" (Galatians 1:8).

Real Life Says . . .

The therapist Carl Rogers believed that every person possesses within himself the answers to his own problems. He did not feel that an outside authority should be imposed upon the one seeking help. In his own words, he writes,

> Experience is, for me, the highest authority. . . . No other person's ideas, and none of my own ideas, are as authoritative as my experience. It is to experience that I must return again and again, to discover a closer approximation to truth as it is in the process of becoming in me. Neither the Bible nor the prophets . . . neither the revelations of God nor man—can take precedence over my own direct experience.

But the Bible says that man's "heart is deceitful above all things and beyond cure. Who can understand it?" (Jeremiah 17:9). If we trust our own experience (our "heart") above the Word of God, we make a major mistake. Our beliefs about life, God and His love for us are to be derived not from our own experience, for the trials we go through may *seem* devoid of His love. We can trust His holy Word above our own experiences, and thereby be on safe and solid ground!

But, Lord . . .

Father, part of the twistedness of sin shows up in my tendency to trust me, instead of You! Although You want me to experience Your love and guidance in this life, You never want me to substitute my perceptions for Your promises. Keep my eyes focused on Your Word today, Lord. In Jesus' name, Amen.

To Ponder . . .

Never deduce truth from experience! Always get your truth from truth! (Stephen Brown)

The Riddle of Reason

We are designed by God to use our minds, not as the final source for what we believe, but as a tool for understanding His perfect Word.

Great men are they that see that spiritual is stronger than any material force, that thoughts rule the world.

(Ralph Waldo Emerson)

Yon Cassias has a lean and hungry look—He thinks too much.

(Shakespeare's *Julius Caesar*)

By setting forth the truth plainly we commend ourselves to every man's conscience in the sight of God. And even if our gospel is veiled, it is veiled to those who are perishing. The god of this age has blinded the minds of unbelievers, so that they cannot see the light of the gospel of the glory of Christ, who is the image of God.

(2 Corinthians 4:2-4)

The Knowledge Nugget

The science fiction writer Robert Heinlein once said, "History does not record anywhere at any time a religion that has any rational basis.

The Absolute Need for an Absolute Authority .... DAY THREE

Religion is a crutch for people not strong enough to stand up to the unknown without help. But, like dandruff, most people do have a religion and spend time and money on it and seem to derive considerable pleasure fiddling with it." Biblical Christianity, contrary to Heinlein's rantings, argues that there is a personal, rational Being who is the Creator of the heavens and the earth. He has made us in His image, and we possess the ability to use our minds, even to argue against Him!

When it comes to the final authority for what we believe, we need to use our reason, but we must beware of falling into a philosophy known as *rationalism*. Rationalism teaches that we should not believe anything which we cannot explain with our finite minds.

One of history's greatest illustrations of rationalism was deism, a philosophical outlook in the eighteenth century which was sometimes called "common-sense religion." One of its most famous exponents was none other than Thomas Jefferson, who took his penknife to those sections of the Bible that he thought were "unreasonable." The Jefferson Bible is still in print today.

God expects us to love Him with our minds (Matthew 22:37), to use the reason He has given us so that we might advance in our understanding of His truths (Ephesians 4:11-16). But our reason must be judged by His Word, rather than the reverse!

Real Life Says . . .

We live in a culture that, on the one hand, exalts experience and emotion to the neglect of logical thinking. On the other hand, it elevates human reason to a position it was never intended to have: as a competing or final authority for what is believed as ultimately true.

The seventeenth-century French mathematician and theologian Blaise Pascal said, "The ultimate purpose of reason is to bring us to the place where we see that there is a limit to reason." The psalmist speaks of the wicked's arrogance: "In his pride the wicked does not seek [God]; in all his thoughts there is no room for God" (Psalm 10:4).

In Second Corinthians 4:2, Paul drives home the point that the clear presentation of truth ought to affect a person's conscience: "By setting forth the truth plainly we commend ourselves to every man's conscience in the sight of God." In the next verses he then emphasizes that for some the gospel makes no sense for two reasons: (1) they are in a perishing condition which "veils" the gospel from their understanding; (2) they are victims of "the god of this age" who gleefully blinds the minds of unbelievers so they will not receive the gospel.

I understand that an Irish farmer was in a local pub, and he offered the following toast to his friend: "When God measures you, may he put the tape around your big and generous heart and not around your small and foolish head." To judge all of reality by our "small and foolish" heads is the great tragedy of rationalism.

But, Lord . . .

Lord, You know how intellectually lazy I can be. I'm also quite capable of believing only those parts of Your Word that pass my mental tests. Forgive my arrogance, Lord. Help me to love You, and Your Word, with my whole mind. In Jesus' name, Amen.

To Ponder . . .

The first duty of a man is not to think for himself, but to think *God's* thoughts after Him.

The Church Crutch

When a Christian's beliefs are determined solely by what his church or his pastor teaches, he is in danger of placing church tradition before God's Word—a mistake made by the Pharisees and clearly condemned by the Lord Jesus.

There was a pastor, himself he cherished,
   who loved his position, not his parish.
So the more he preached,
   the less he reached,
and this is why his parish perished.

(Anonymous)

Alone I cannot serve the Lord effectively, and he will spare no pains to teach me this. He will bring things to an end, allowing doors to close and leaving me ineffectively knocking my head against a wall until I realize that I need the help of the Body as well as of the Lord.

(Watchman Nee)

You have a fine way of setting aside the commands of God in order to observe your own traditions! . . . You nullify the word of God by your tradition that you have handed down. And you do many things like that.

(Mark 7:9, 13)

DAY FOUR .... *The Absolute Need for an Absolute Authority*

The Knowledge Nugget

A church that was looking for a new pastor had many older members who were hoping that a seasoned, experienced minister would be chosen. Instead, the search committee recommended a young man, fresh out of seminary, with the hope that he might breathe some fresh life into the congregation. After the pastor had been chosen, one man commented to an older member that this marked the beginning of better things for the church. "Yes," the elderly man replied with a wry smile. "Moving on to greener pastors."

Several devotionals in Section One have set the stage for today's discussion. In the Day 13 devotional ("Do You Feel the Need for a Creed?"), we saw that we should be thankful for those who have attempted to put into brief statements the fundamental beliefs of the Christian faith. Sometimes our rituals or rites lose their meaning and must be brought back into conformity with God's Word (as we saw in Day 16, "The Right Rites"). We can make the mistake of caring too little or too much for our traditions, as we pointed out in the Day 19 devotional, "Sacred Cows Make Gourmet Burgers!"

It is certainly not wrong to listen to one's pastor (even if he is "greener") or other, more mature believers in the Christian congregation. What *is* wrong is to let those individuals do your thinking for you.

If the Bible is our final authority for what we believe, then we will use it to evaluate our creeds, our practices and our lives. When Martin Luther and other Reformation leaders questioned the need for a pope who would interpret God's truth for the people, they got into a lot of trouble. In fact, those who opposed the Reformers said that they had substituted a "paper pope" (the Bible) for the real one!

Real Life Says . . .

Many in our culture don't want to be told what to believe. Man's autonomy (being a law to himself) resists the truth of God, whether that authority is shown in an organization like the church or in a book like the Bible.

For the evangelical Christian, the question of one's final authority is a critical one. As much as we would like to think that no tradition or church decision will ever compete with the Bible's authority, we need to remind ourselves that we are not all that different from the Pharisees of Jesus' day.

When His disciples were challenged by the Pharisees for not living according to the "tradition of the elders," Jesus minced no words in confronting the religious leaders of Israel with the fact that their traditions had supplanted the Word of God. He quotes Isaiah's prophecy, stating that Isaiah had written about "you hypocrites"! Isaiah wrote: "These people honor me with their lips, but their hearts are far from me. They worship me in vain; their teachings are but rules taught by men" (Mark 7:6-7). Jesus concludes, "You have a fine way of setting aside the commands of God in order to observe your own traditions! . . . Thus you nullify the word of God by your tradition that you have handed down" (7:9, 13).

But, Lord . . .

Father, You know my tendency to be a "man-follower." Help me to learn from others and to honor the church traditions which have the blessing of Your Word. But don't allow me to substitute anything or anyone for Your Word. In Jesus' name, Amen.

To Ponder . . .

The church can greatly assist me to know God's truth, but it must be tested by the Scriptures.

Being a Berean Believer

Even the excellent teaching of respected men and women of God must be tested by the conformity of their teaching to the written Word of God, the Bible.

A great number of people don't have a right to their own opinion because they don't know what they're talking about.

(Andy Rooney)

Every man is entitled to be wrong in his opinions. But no man is entitled to be wrong in his facts.

(Anonymous)

Now the Bereans were of more noble character than the Thessalonians, for they received the message with great eagerness and examined the Scriptures every day to see if what Paul said was true.

(Acts 17:11)

The Knowledge Nugget

The nineteenth-century poet and essayist Heinrich Hinde was with a friend, standing in front of a wonderful cathedral in Paris. "Why don't they build buildings like this anymore?" the friend asked.

The Absolute Need for an Absolute Authority .... DAY FIVE

Hinde replied, "My dear friend, in those days people had convictions. Today we only have opinions—and you don't build cathedrals with opinions."

As we see in today's passage, no human's opinion, even the esteemed Apostle Paul's, is enough. The Berean believers are noted in the Bible for being noble precisely in that they examined the teachings of Paul on the basis of what the Scriptures said.

I come from the great state of North Carolina, a state which has produced Michael Jordan, the first successful flying machine (the Wright Brothers' plane, *not* Michael Jordan!), Pepsi-Cola and Dr. Billy Graham. Imagine with me that Dr. Graham has come to your midweek church service and agrees to speak to the congregation. I suspect that many would make sure the sound guy tapes Dr. Graham's talk. Some would quickly call their friends to invite them to church and many might rush home to get their cameras (perhaps missing Dr. Graham's talk altogether). But how many would analyze his message to make sure it was consistent with the Word of God? We might even think it rude and impolite to do such "critical listening," but that's what it means to be a Berean believer. Our own opinions often need to be changed by God's truth. William Blake once stated, "The man who never alters his opinion is like standing water, and breeds reptiles of the mind."

Our only dependable authority not only in what we are to believe, but also in how we are to live our lives, is the written Word of God, the Bible. Mark Twain, a man who gave no evidence of being a follower of Jesus Christ, rightly commented, "Loyalty to petrified opinion never yet broke a chain or freed a human soul." But history's highway is littered with broken chains that once bound people in sin who are now free because of the authoritative Word of God.

Real Life Says . . .

We live in a celebrity-obsessed society that seems to have lost any ability to discern truth from error. Christians must be aware of the danger of hero-worship, of substituting the thoughts of men for the truths of God. And that determination not to allow anyone else to do our thinking for us, or to permit the substitution of others' opinions for what the Word truly teaches, does not come naturally to us. We must constantly guard ourselves—and educate ourselves—in the Bible, lest we become petrified ourselves! Berean believers are marked by both an eagerness to be taught and a commitment to compare what is heard with God's unerring Word. Their examination of the Scriptures was *daily*. Eagerness to learn the truth and a diligence in examining the Word of God are not mutually exclusive activities.

Proverbs 18:2 says that "a fool finds no pleasure in understanding but delights in airing his own opinions." In a culture that confuses opinions with truth and shuns critical examination, people today desperately need the dependable Word of God as their authority in all matters of life.

But, Lord . . .

Father, I know that it's going to take some work to start living as a Berean believer. Help me not to take the well-worn path of those who believe all that they hear. Guide me by Your Spirit to focus on Your truth so that I may encourage Your messengers. In Jesus' name, Amen.

To Ponder . . .

Are you building the cathedral of your life with your convictions from the Bible, the Word of God?

What Kind of Dirt Are You?

Receptivity to the Word of God is judged by the fruit of one's life.

A salty pagan, full of the juices of life, is a hundred times dearer to God, and also far more attractive to men, than a scribe who knows his Bible . . . in whom none of this results in repentance, action, and above all, death of the self. A terrible curse hangs over the know-it-all who does nothing.

(Helmut Thielicke)

A woman said her mother was not a gardener, but was planting seeds when her daughter dropped by to visit. The rows were not very straight, and the daughter suggested that her mother mark each row so that she would know what she had planted. The mother replied, "My dear girl, this is a garden, not a cemetery. I expect all of these seeds to come up and identify themselves."

(Cecile Broccolo)

Still other seed fell on good soil. It came up and yielded a crop, a hundred times more than was sown. . . . The seed on good soil stands for those with a noble and good heart, who hear the word, retain it, and by persevering produce a crop.

(Luke 8:8, 15)

The Knowledge Nugget

How does one know whether he is responding correctly to the Word of God? Jesus gives us the parable of the sower, which might better be called the parable of the soils. A farmer indiscriminately scatters seed in four locations: along the path, on rocky land, on thorny ground and on good soil. The farmer spreads his seed by swinging his arm in a circular fashion (called "broadcasting"); the seed lands where it lands. The seed does not determine whether it grows; *the place where it lands* determines whether the seed comes up and yields a crop.

The seed sown along the path is trampled under foot. The birds swoop down and feast on it. Jesus tells us that this surface represents those who merely hear the Word of God, but are victims of "the devil [who] comes and takes away the word from their hearts, so that they may not believe and be saved" (8:12).

The seed sown on rocky land comes up, but the plants wither from a lack of moisture. This surface stands for those who receive the word ("with joy," Jesus says), but because they have no root, these temporary believers fall away in a time of testing (8:13).

The seed which is scattered among thorns doesn't have a chance. This surface represents those who hear the word, but "are choked by life's worries, riches and pleasures, and they do not mature" (8:14).

The fourth surface is the only successful one. Assuming that the seed is sown equally among the four surfaces, this farmer's percentage of success is only twenty-five percent! But the seed scattered on good soil comes up, yields "a crop, a hundred times more than was sown" (8:8). This surface represents those with a noble and good heart, who hear the word and retain it, "and by persevering produce a crop" (8:15). Note that success is not easily achieved; it requires *perseverance*.

Real Life Says . . .

One would think that our pragmatic world would love this parable. After all, everybody esteems a productive person, and the "good soil" produces such a result that the farmer's "wasted seed" (the seventy-five percent that produced no positive result) is more than made up by the hundredfold success of the good soil.

The rub comes with Jesus' conclusion that all who hear His word fall into one of these four categories. The key is to figure out what kind of soil one is so that the seed will take root and produce a God-honoring crop.

When we had to get topsoil delivered to our yard, neighbors warned me that some topsoil companies were delivering gophers as a bonus with their soil! I asked the old man who sold us our topsoil if he knew it was good, gopher-free soil. He said, "I've been in dirt for thirty years, Mr. Dixon, and this is the best I've got!" Is the topsoil of your life the best you've got?

But, Lord . . .

Father, great Farmer of my heart, grant me a receptivity to Your Word which will not waste Your time, nor fail to produce an honorable crop. In Jesus' name, Amen.

To Ponder . . .

When it comes to soil analysis, we can know *ourselves* by the crop we produce!

The Bible Is Not a Systematic Theology Book, Thank the Lord!

Although the Bible is not a systematic theology textbook, we ought to pursue its doctrines in a logical way so that all of God's truth can be learned and applied to our lives and our world.

In writing his thirteen volumes of theology, Karl Barth commented, "Every time I come out with a new book of dogmatics, the angels start giggling that 'old Barth's trying to explain God again!' "

A little girl was reading the Bible in an airport. A man asked her, "Little girl, do you believe everything you read in that book?"

"Yes sir," she said.

"You mean you believe that Jonah was swallowed by a whale?!"

"Yes sir, if that's what the Bible says, then I believe it. And I'll ask Jonah about it when I get to heaven."

"But what if Jonah's not in heaven?" the man asked rudely.

"Then," said the young girl sweetly, "you can ask him."

Sanctify them by the truth; your word is truth.

(John 17:17)

The Absolute Need for an Absolute Authority .... DAY SEVEN

The Knowledge Nugget

The discipline known as *systematic theology* takes the doctrinal material of the Bible and arranges that material into logical categories. So if one wanted to know what the Bible had to say about, for example, the deity of Jesus Christ, one could begin at Genesis and read all the way through the book of Revelation, making notes on every text that said something about the deity of Jesus. If that person were to organize his notes into an outline on the subject of the deity of Christ (the attributes of Jesus, the divine names of Jesus, the divine works of Jesus, etc.), he would be taking a systematic theology approach to that important subject. Although there are many books which claim to provide a complete systematic theology on an issue like the deity of Christ, personal study of all those passages is still a worthwhile endeavor because some theology books might miss important passages or be flawed by certain doctrinal opinions.

Then why did God not give us His Word as a systematic theology textbook? Have you looked at any theology textbooks recently? They are often dry, complicated and sometimes confusing. What bothers me most of all is that none have any cartoons. And precious few show any sense of humor!

God gave us His many truths in a book, but, thankfully, not in a theology book! This is not to say that theology books are unimportant or unhelpful. A good theology book will boil down the vital issues of a doctrine so that it can be understood, defended and coordinated with other doctrines.

When we look at the Bible, we see the doctrines of the Christian faith illustrated in the lives of Israel, the early church and individual believers. "Illustrated" may not be the best term, for often we see the truths of God *violated* or *ignored* in the lives of Israel, the early church and individual believers! But we can learn from negative examples as well.

Real Life Says . . .

For many in our culture, the Bible is a collection of religious stories and musings that have little if any relevance to life in the twenty-first century. Viewing biblical characters as "prescientific," many people today find it difficult to identify with Moses or David or Ananias and Sapphira.

The problem is not the Bible, but biblical illiteracy. Anyone who seriously studies the characters and events of the Bible will discover that the same trials and temptations that tormented Samson, King David or Simon Peter sneak up on us. The doctrines of the Bible are given within the warp and woof of everyday life. (If you're like me, you had to look up "warp and woof." The "warp" are those threads that run lengthwise in a fabric; the "woof" are those that run crosswise.)

God communicates His truths through the fabric of the lives of biblical characters and events. It may, for example, involve work to find the doctrine of God's *omnipresence* (His being everywhere) in Solomon's prayer dedicating the temple in First Kings 8, or discovering the deity of the Holy Spirit in the story of hypocritical Ananias and Sapphira in Acts 5, but it will be worth it!

But, Lord . . .

Father, the variety of Your Word astounds me. Guide me as I search for Your truths in the people and events of the two testaments. In Jesus' name, Amen.

To Ponder . . .

What theology is God teaching through the fabric of your life?

A Needlepoint of Knowledge—Part 1: Incredible Craftsmanship!

Today's Focus

The Bible is the most practical book in the world, a truth made abundantly clear in Psalm 119.

Ignorance of the Scriptures is ignorance of Christ.

(Jerome)

The Bible is alive, it speaks to me; it has feet, it runs after me; it has hands, it lays hold on me.

(Martin Luther)

Direct me in the path of your commands,
    for there I find delight. . . .
Your decrees are the theme of my song
    wherever I lodge.

(Psalm 119:35, 54)

The Knowledge Nugget

Psalm 119 is the longest psalm in the book of Psalms, and each stanza exalts the Word of God. You may be using a Bible that divides the psalm into sections, with each section of seven to eight verses headed by a Hebrew letter (such as "aleph" or "beth," etc.). Psalm 119 is an *acrostic*; each succeeding stanza begins with the next Hebrew letter in the alphabet, for a total of twenty-two stanzas.

Why is this important? Psalm 119 reveals the *craftsmanship* of the psalmist as he extols the Word of the living God. He took time and expended great energy in this literary work. I am reminded of the former NFL football great, Rosie Grier, a monster of a man, who *needlepointed* in his spare time as he prepared for his next game. If it's manly to needlepoint, it's certainly manly to spend time in God's Word!

The Word of God is the key to keeping a young man pure, to silencing the enemies of God and to revealing the goodness of the Lord. It provides peace, strength, sustenance, wisdom, fulfillment, confidence and a restful night's sleep; it will develop faithfulness, inspire praise and grant guidance in making right choices. All these promises are in Psalm 119; read it and find the verses yourself.

Roger Miklos, one of the world's foremost modern-day treasure hunters, said, "A very conservative estimate of the treasure still lost off the U.S. coast between North Carolina and Florida is enough to put $1 million in the pocket of every man, woman and child living in New York City." The obvious question is: Why not give the money to *me*? But the point of this illustration is clear: the treasures awaiting each of us in the Word of God must be *mined*. If I want them to be mine, that is.

Real Life Says . . .

The writer Frederick Buechner put into words what many in our culture feel about the Bible:

> In short, one way to describe the Bible, written by many different men over a period of three thousand years and more, would be to say that it is a disorderly collection of sixty-odd books which are often tedious, barbaric, obscure, and teem with contradictions and inconsistencies. It is a swarming

compost of a book, an Irish stew of poetry and propaganda, law and legalism, myth and murk, history and hysteria.

Many in our culture think of the Bible as an interesting collection of the musings of religious people. Instead of seeing the Word of God as God's inerrant communication to His creation, many think it is *man's* collection of thoughts about God.

Certainly God used the personalities, intelligence and writing styles of the biblical writers in communicating His eternal truths. And despite the proverb "To err is human," the fact that God used human beings in that work does not mean that there must be errors in the Word of God. In fact, the Bible teaches that the Holy Spirit "carried along" the writers of Scripture, protecting them from miscommunicating God's message (2 Peter 1:21).

Contrary to Buechner's view, the Bible is not "an Irish stew of poetry and propaganda." Although it is marked by great variety, it is a carefully crafted communiqué from the Creator Himself!

But, Lord . . .

Lord, I thank You for the sheer variety of Your Word. And I praise You for using the life of David, who took the time to be led by Your Spirit in penning Psalm 119. Slow me down, Lord, that my life might be so crafted by Your truth. In Jesus' name, Amen.

To Ponder . . .

What is the needlepoint God is making of *your* life from His Word?

A Needlepoint of Knowledge—Part 2: "Who Wants to Be . . . Really Rich?"

The studied obedience of the Word of God brings true riches. And unlike the wealth of this world, this kind of prosperity does not fade away, but lasts for eternity.

Prosperity knits a man to the world. He feels that he is "finding his place in it," while really it is finding its place in him.

(C.S. Lewis)

The most miserable person in the world is not the person who doesn't have what he wants, but the person who has what he wants and has found out that it doesn't make any difference.

(Corrie ten Boom)

I rejoice in following your statutes
    as one rejoices in great riches.

(Psalm 119:14)

The Knowledge Nugget

The comedienne Phyllis Diller once said, "I want my children to have all the things I never could afford. Then I want to move in with them!" We are a very wealthy society. One study asks the question, "Are you wealthy enough to have 840 servants?" Everett Hafner, a physicist, indicates that such would be the equivalent in manpower to the machines, appliances and industrial processes used by the average family today. Some of the work-savers include the family car (equal to 132 servants), a central heating system (equal to 100 servants), a water heater (equal to 20 servants), an oven and refrigerator (also equal to 20 servants) and chemicals and textiles (equal to 100 servants)! We are wealthy indeed.

I must confess that I have occasionally watched TV programs like "Who Wants to Be a Millionaire?" One thing that impresses me is how contestants react when they start making some real money (say, $32,000) and then miss a question. Their "lifeline" didn't know the answer, the audience was no help at all, and they used their "50-50" to eliminate two of the answers—*and they still got it wrong!* And that was their "final answer"! They take their consolation prize, smile and shake Regis' hand. I think I would make a scene by complaining that the question was too hard, or my friend was too stupid or the audience too dense! But they just take the money, smile and walk offstage.

It would be fascinating to find out what happens to the contestants after the show is over—especially to the ones who become millionaires. Perhaps like a lot of lottery winners, their lives do not become happier or more fulfilled when their bank accounts start to burst at the seams. That's because human beings were never intended to find their deepest joy in possessions. Or, as humorist Art Buchwald puts it, "The best things in life aren't things."

I understand that Hetty Green went down in history as "America's greatest miser." When she died she left an estate of over $100 million. But she ate cold oatmeal because it cost money to heat it. Her son lost a leg because she delayed so long looking for a free clinic. She was wealthy but lived as a pauper.

Real Life Says . . .

Many in our world would love to win the lottery or score big on a million-dollar game show. But God's Word warns us, "Though your riches increase, do not set your heart on them" (Psalm 62:10). Paul instructs Timothy, "Command those who are rich in this present world not to be arrogant nor to put their hope in wealth, which is so uncertain, but to put their hope in God, who richly provides us with everything for our enjoyment" (1 Timothy 6:17).

True wealth, Psalm 119 tells us, comes from knowing and obeying God's commands: "I rejoice in following your statutes as one rejoices in great riches" (119:14). And Jesus says,

> Do not store up for yourselves treasures on earth, where moth and rust destroy, and where thieves break in and steal. But store up for yourselves treasures in heaven, where moth and rust do not destroy, and where thieves do not break in and steal. For where your treasure is, there your heart will be also. (Matthew 6:19-21)

But, Lord . . .

Father, protect my heart from earthbound treasures. And give me joy in obeying Your eternal Word! In Jesus' name, Amen.

To Ponder . . .

When I have any money, I get rid of it as quickly as possible, lest it find a way into my heart. (John Wesley)

A Needlepoint of Knowledge—Part 3: Strength for Suffering

The Word of God provides strength for enduring the trials and tribulations of life. God's promises and precepts are to be the refuge of the believer when life's difficulties come.

If science is your religion, what do you do with your pain?

> (A Buddhist to his American friend)

Suffering is meant not only to burn out the dross, but to burn in the promises.

> (C.H. Spurgeon)

It was good for me to be afflicted
    so that I might learn your decrees. . . .

I know, O LORD, that your laws are righteous,
    and in faithfulness you have afflicted me.

> (Psalm 119:71, 75)

The Knowledge Nugget

A woman, recovering from knee surgery and the extraction of impacted wisdom teeth, was lying on the couch with an ice bag on her leg and hot water bottles against both cheeks. "From the kitchen," she says, "I heard my mother cry out in pain. Through a mouth stuffed with gauze I asked her what had happened. 'You know,' she replied, 'there's nothing worse than a paper cut!'"

The Word of God has much to say to the believer about suffering. Isaiah declares that it can actually be a positive experience: "Surely it was for my benefit that I suffered such anguish" (Isaiah 38:17). The incarnate Son of God experienced the full range of human suffering; Hebrews says about Christ, "Although he was a son, he learned obedience from what he suffered" (Hebrews 5:8). In an astounding passage, the Apostle Paul says to the Philippian believers, "It has been granted to you on behalf of Christ not only to believe on him, but also to suffer for him" (Philippians 1:29).

The viewpoint known as "prosperity theology" has done much damage in the church, convincing many Christians that, as Jerry Savelle, one of its advocates, says, "It is not the will of God that anyone be sick with any sickness or disease or pain whatever—from hangnails to tuberculosis." Such a ridiculous statement does not square with the whole counsel of God. (Note passages such as the book of Job; 2 Corinthians 12:1-10; 1 Timothy 5:23; 1 Peter 2:21, etc.) Much of the "health and wealth" gospel can be dismissed as just another verse of Carly Simon's song, "I haven't got time for the pain!"

Real Life Says . . .

Many, perhaps most, in our culture want to avoid suffering at all costs. But the Word of God has been given to strengthen the believer to endure suffering. Pain is often used by God, C.S. Lewis reminds us, "to rouse a deaf world."

Rather than denying the reality of pain and suffering, the biblical writers acknowledge God's providential hand in the difficulties of life. For example, in a different psalm, David writes, "For you, O God, tested us; you refined us like silver. You brought us into prison and laid burdens on our backs. You let men ride over our heads; we went through fire and water, but you brought us to a place of abundance" (Psalm 66:10-12). While Christians often blame Satan for the problems of life, Hosea says,

> Come, let us return to the LORD.
> He has torn us to pieces
>   but he will heal us;
> he has injured us
>   but he will bind up our wounds.
> After two days he will revive us;
>   on the third day he will restore us,
>   that we may live in his presence.
> Let us acknowledge the LORD;
>   let us press on to acknowledge him. (Hosea 6:1-3)

The psalmist praises God for the difficulties of life: "It was good for me to be afflicted so that I might learn your decrees. . . . I know, O LORD, that your laws are righteous, and in faithfulness you have afflicted me" (Psalm 119:71, 75). Peter echoes this same perspective: "To this you were called, because Christ suffered for you, leaving you an example, that you should follow in his steps" (1 Peter 2:21).

But, Lord . . .

Father, I know that I am not to seek suffering. But when the trials of life come, please encourage me by Your Spirit that I might be in a teachable mood, so that I may learn Your decrees. In Jesus' name, Amen.

To Ponder . . .

There's never been a pit so deep that He is not deeper still. (Corrie ten Boom)

Talk about Relevant!

The Bible is the most relevant book in the world, for it gives us the mind of God, teaching us how to live life for God.

It's almost impossible to overestimate the unimportance of most things.

(John Logue)

Do not try to make the Bible relevant; its relevance is axiomatic.

(Dietrich Bonhoeffer)

For the grace of God that brings salvation has appeared to all men. It teaches us to say "No" to ungodliness and worldly passions, and to live self-controlled, upright and godly lives in this present age.

(Titus 2:11-12)

The Knowledge Nugget

A tourist who could rightly be called an "ugly American" was walking down the street in a tropical country when he saw a man sitting under a palm tree, reading the Bible. "My good man," the tourist said with laughter, "in my country that book is out of date!" The native looked up and, with as much tact as he could muster, said to the

American, "My good man, if this book were out of date here, *you would have been eaten by now!*"

If the Bible and the Bible alone is the authoritative Word of God, then C.S. Lewis' comment can be easily applied to it: "All that is not eternal is eternally out of date." Jesus clearly taught that "heaven and earth will pass away, but my words will never pass away" (Matthew 24:35). The term "relevant" means "related to the matter at hand, to the point." If the question is how this life should be lived, then the Bible is the *most relevant* book in the world!

Sometimes we Christians are relevant, but to the wrong generation. The fine Christian writer Leith Anderson calls us to a biblical balance in his book *Dying for Change*:

> In the commendable effort to be relevant we must be diligent students of people and trends. We must speak the language of our generation and constantly update our ministries to be effective. Because the required effort is great, there may be a temptation to neglect the spiritual. To do so is to tear the heart out of Christian ministry and lower the work of the gospel to something less than supernatural. The uncompromising balance must be maintained, forfeiting neither relevance nor revelation.

Real Life Says . . .

In the minds of many today, the Bible is merely a collection of ancient religious graffiti. It is suitable for older folk who are getting ready to go to heaven and for children in Sunday school. For the self-made man or woman of today, the Bible seems to offer little of value or relevance.

The problem with this position, of course, is that it is simply not true. The Word of God speaks to every issue of human experience, providing case studies of those who followed God and were blessed, and of those who chose their own way and perished.

The Apostle Paul's words to Titus are "to the point" here. He writes: "For the grace of God that brings salvation has appeared to all men. It teaches us to say 'No' to ungodliness and worldly passions, and to live self-controlled, upright and godly lives in this present age" (Titus 2:11-12). The expression "in this present age" literally reads in the Greek "in the *now* world." The teachings of the Word of God prepare us for life in *this* world, as well as in the next.

Outside the city of Atlanta is a megachurch whose name is "The Church in the Now!" I don't know the story of how they picked that particular name, but I suspect those Christians had *had it* with the opinion that biblical Christianity is irrelevant to today's world. Have you? Then get into the Word of God and discover its relevance for yourself.

But, Lord . . .

Lord, I praise You that Your Word is by no means "out-of-date." Sometimes the way we treat Your Word, or even the translations we use, can cause some to think that it is not "to the point" regarding this life. Please correct that wrong thinking by Your truth. In Jesus' name, Amen.

To Ponder . . .

If "relevance" means "to the point," then how do we help others to get back to the main point of life: living for Christ?

Being Closed Is Not Necessarily a Bad Thing

When we speak of the "canon" of Scripture, we are referring to the belief that only the sixty-six books of the Bible meet the criteria (rule or "canon") for being considered the inspired Word of God.

We believe the Bible to be the word of God, as far as it is translated correctly; we also believe the Book of Mormon to be the word of God.

(Joseph Smith)

In my opinion, every book of the New Testament was written by a baptized Jew between the forties and eighties of the first century A.D. (very probably sometime between about A.D. 50 and 75).

(W.F. Albright)

I have treasured the words of his
> mouth more than my daily bread.

(Job 23:12)

The Knowledge Nugget

When we discussed the issue of one's final religious authority in the Day 1 devotional of this section ("Where Did You Get *That*

Idea?"), we noted four sources from which people derive their beliefs: experience, reason, church tradition and revelation. Evangelical Christians are not alone in claiming that they have received special revelation from God; others also claim it of their holy books.

The Mormons have *The Book of Mormon*, a collection of stories supposedly given to Joseph Smith by the angel Moroni. (Remember what Paul said in Galatians 1:8? "But even if we or an angel from heaven should preach a gospel other than the one we preached to you, let him be eternally condemned!") Those who belong to the cult known as Christian Science believe that Mary Baker Eddy was God's prophetess and revere her book, *Science and Health with Key to the Scriptures*. Although the Jehovah's Witnesses say that only the Bible is the Word of God, they treat their organization's material as the final authority for what they believe and practice.

Other sacred books which compete with the Bible include *The Divine Principle* (the authority of the Unification Church), *The Bhagavad Gita* (a sacred Hindu text) and the *Koran* (the cherished guidebook of 1.2 billion Muslims worldwide). It could safely be said that every literate cultural group in the world has its divine books.

When we talk about the "canon" of Scripture, we are referring to the question of what books ought to be considered the Word of God. The specific criteria that need to be met for a book to be considered part of God's Scriptures include authorship by an apostle or an associate of an apostle, acceptance in the churches, recognition and use by the church fathers (the scholars of the first eight centuries of the Christian Church), consistency with the rest of God's Word, the ability of the book to edify (build up) the church, evidence of the witness of the Spirit in the book, etc.

Canonicity involves both *inclusion* and *exclusion*. By "inclusion" we mean that no books which are truly of God have been left out of our Bibles. Although the authenticity of books like Second Peter and James were debated for a while in the church, ultimately they were seen as from God. By "exclusion" we mean that those books that claimed to be of God (but were not) did not make their way into the canon of Scripture. Books like *The Shepherd of Hermas* were respected in the early church, but were later understood not to be divinely inspired. Protestant Christians reject the fourteen apocryphal books (included in Catholic Bibles) as being divinely inspired, although they give interesting historical information about the time period between the Old and New Testaments.

Real Life Says . . .

This whole discussion makes little sense to our culture, for most do not believe that God has communicated to His creation through a book. And they feel that all religious traditions are equally valid.

The Old Testament's canonicity was certainly clear by the time of Jesus (see Luke 24:27, 44). The New Testament's canonicity seems to have taken a while, but there is evidence that by 200 A.D. it was also settled. When we say we believe in a "closed" canon, we mean that no additional books are to be expected which should be added to the sixty-six books of the Old and New Testaments. God's special revelation of His will and mind to humanity is completed in what we now have in the Bible. The believer in Christ has every reason to say with Job, "I have treasured the words of his mouth more than my daily bread" (Job 23:12).

But, Lord . . .

Father, this is fairly complicated stuff. But I want to recognize Your authority in the sixty-six books of the Word of God, and stand for Your truth in this needy world. In Jesus' name, Amen.

To Ponder . . .

The Word of God is either absolute or obsolete. (Vance Havner)

The Voice of God
No One Can Escape

Today's Focus

By the term "general revelation," we mean God's communication of some of His truths to all people everywhere through creation, human nature and history.

If you wish to make an apple pie from scratch, you must first invent the universe.

(Carl Sagan)

Labor to keep alive in your breast that little spark of celestial fire called Conscience.

(George Washington)

The wrath of God is being revealed from heaven against all the godlessness and wickedness of men who suppress the truth by their wickedness, since what may be known about God is plain to them, because God has made it plain to them. For since the creation of the world God's invisible qualities—his eternal power and divine nature—have been clearly seen, being understood from what has been made, so that men are without excuse.

(Romans 1:18-20)

The Knowledge Nugget

Woody Allen once said that "The universe is merely a fleeting idea in God's mind—a pretty uncomfortable thought, particularly if you've just made a down payment on a house." When we speak of general revelation, we are acknowledging that creation is not a fleeting idea in God's mind. God has communicated truth about Himself to all people at all times through creation (nature), human nature (especially conscience), and history. The cosmologist (a person who holds a view about the origin of the universe) Allan Sandage once commented,

> Science cannot answer the deepest questions. As soon as you ask why there is something instead of nothing, you have gone beyond science. I find it quite improbable that such order came out of chaos. There has to be some organizing principle. God to me is the explanation for the miracle of existence—why there is something instead of nothing.

The issue was quite simple for the psalmist: "The heavens declare the glory of God; the skies proclaim the work of his hands" (Psalm 19:1). When my family and I lived in northern Canada, we were treated each year to the phenomenon known as the aurora borealis, or the Northern Lights. The earth's gravitational pull produces electrical charges which result in an incredible light show. Such wonders are God's way of speaking to us through "the work of His hands."

Human nature is another avenue of God's communication to all people at all times. Because all human beings are made in the image of God, it is impossible for any to escape their own nature completely. Although our consciences are not perfect, they remind us of morals and values which we often violate (see Romans 2). Sometimes called "God's early warning system," the conscience is a powerful moral proof of God's laws. A mother, helping her son with his spelling assignment, came to the words "conscious" and "conscience." When she asked him if he knew the difference between the two, he responded, "Sure, Mom. 'Conscious' is when you are aware of some-thing and 'conscience' is when you wish you weren't."

The third avenue of God's communication to all people at all times is human history. Ambrose Bierce defined history as "an account, mostly false, of events, mostly unimportant, which are brought about by rulers, mostly knaves, and soldiers, mostly fools." The Bible, however, declares that "the Most High God is sovereign over the kingdoms of men and sets over them anyone he wishes" (Daniel 5:21).

Real Life Says . . .

This world explains away creation by the much-flawed theory of evolution. It therefore fails to recognize the human being as God's image-bearer. Many also try to dismiss the gift of conscience by sug-gesting that it is merely sociologically determined. The idea that his-tory is "His story," that *God* is in control of the affairs of men and nations, seems ludicrous to this lost world.

The Apostle Paul makes it quite clear that men and women suppress the truth of God's existence and divine nature as proclaimed in creation. And they are "without excuse" for turning a deaf ear to the voice of God (Romans 1). How human—and how wrong—to try to deny the voice of God that seeks to convince us of our need for forgiveness.

But, Lord . . .

Father, thank You for the universe—made with Your hands. Open my ears to hear Your voice through Your creation. In Jesus' name, Amen.

To Ponder . . .

God made the world and no one else has the recipe to make an-other. (*What Children Say about God*)

The Voice of God Some Never Hear

By the term "special revelation," we are referring to God's communication of Himself and His mind to some people at particular times and places. The two avenues of God's special revelation are His written Word, the Bible, and the Living Word, the Lord Jesus Christ.

Scripture is the library of the Holy Ghost.

(Thomas Watson)

God's revelation in nature may be likened to a great concert or symphony. Some hear only the instruments. But those who are familiar with the composer and know the words hear more than the music. In much the same way, only the one who has a personal relationship with the Creator through Jesus Christ can really see in nature the fullness of what God intended to communicate through it.

(R.P. Lightner)

How, then, can they call on the one they have not believed in? And how can they believe in the one of whom they have not heard? And how can they hear without someone preaching to them? And how can they preach unless they are sent? As it is written, "How beautiful are the feet of those who bring good news!"

(Romans 10:14-15)

DAY FOURTEEN .... *The Absolute Need for an Absolute Authority*

The Knowledge Nugget

We noted in our discussion of general revelation that God has communicated certain truths about Himself through creation, human nature and history. Every human being has the ability to deduce from creation the existence of an infinite God. Every person has within himself the testimony of God's moral nature in the fallible form of a conscience. And this Creator has not remained distant from His creation. He has gotten involved in the affairs of men and nations, leaving a witness of His intervention in history.

While the witness of general revelation cannot save a person, it shows mankind's knowledge, and rejection, of basic truths about God (Romans 1-2). Only special revelation can bring salvation. God has communicated His will and mind finally and ultimately through His Son and through His completed Word, the Bible.

A five-year-old girl disobeyed her mother and was sent to her room. Later, the mother talked with her about what she had done. Teary-eyed, the child asked, "Why do we do wrong things, Mommy?"

"Well," the mom said, "sometimes the devil tells us to do something wrong and we listen to him. We need to listen to God instead."

To which the little girl replied, "But God doesn't talk loud enough!"

In Christ, God's Word come to earth (John 1); the Lord Jesus is God the Father speaking loudly and clearly. He not only affirmed the authority of the Old Testament, but also put His own words on an equal footing (see Matthew 5). He predicted the coming of the New Testament through the apostles, who would be guided by the Holy Spirit (see John 14:26).

Real Life Says . . .

Some might say that if God is to be believed at all, He must communicate His mind and will equally clearly to all human beings. That is not the path God has chosen. In the Old Testament He selected a particular nation (Israel) to be a witness to other nations that "all the peoples on earth [would] be blessed through [Abraham]" (Genesis 12:3). In the New Testament, God came Himself (in the person of His Son) to proclaim the kingdom of heaven. That "Word became flesh and made his dwelling among us" (John 1:14).

The Church has been called by God to spread the gospel so that those who have not heard will hear the message of salvation in Christ, for people need to hear in order to believe (Romans 10). That means that someone must care enough to preach or share the truth about Jesus Christ with them.

But, Lord . . .

Father, there are many things I don't understand about those who have not received Your special revelation. What I do know is that I have the responsibility to spread the gospel of Your Son to those who have yet to hear His name or see a Bible. Help me to be Your instrument today so that the music of both general and special revelation may begin in some new hearts. In Jesus' name, Amen.

To Ponder . . .

"When your words came, I ate them; they were my joy and my heart's delight." (Jeremiah 15:16)

Not Waiting to Exhale

The doctrine of inspiration refers to the "out-breathing" or exhaling of God's truth through His chosen and protected instruments. If the Bible is the "God-breathed" revelation of God, then its trustworthiness is assured.

I am a Christian because God says so, and I did what He told me to do, and I stand on God's Word, and if the Book goes down, I'll go with it.

(Billy Sunday)

Inspiration was not God magically transcending human minds and faculties: it was God expressing His will through the dedication of human minds and faculties. It does not supersede the sacred writer's own personality and make him God's machine: it reinforces his personality and makes him God's living witness.

(James S. Stewart)

All Scripture is God-breathed and is useful for teaching, rebuking, correcting and training in righteousness, so that the man of God may be thoroughly equipped for every good work.

(2 Timothy 3:16-17)

The Knowledge Nugget

The doctrine of inspiration teaches that the Holy Spirit guided certain men, using their backgrounds, education, experience, intelligence, writing styles, etc., to record what God wanted communicated without error. Several terms are used in theology to describe various aspects of this critical doctrine: *infallible* means that the Scriptures are incapable of teaching deception; *inerrant* means that what was written is not liable to be proven false or mistaken; *plenary* means that inspiration extends to all parts of the Bible alike; and *verbal* means that the actual language form used was divinely directed. When Christians say they believe in the "verbal, plenary, infallible, inerrant Scriptures," they are saying a mouthful!

Although opinions on the doctrine of inspiration are numerous, and there are very important questions to discuss, we believe that the Bible we presently possess has come from a thoroughly trustworthy God who used—and protected—chosen individuals to record His truth. These human writers were the recipients of the out-breathing of God Himself, as Paul tells Timothy that "all Scripture is God-breathed and is useful . . ." (2 Timothy 3:16).

Evangelical Christians do not believe that the writers of Holy Scripture were typewriters upon whom God banged out His Word. John MacArthur directs our attention to the Holy Spirit's work in inspiration when he says,

> When Paul sat down and wrote his epistles, the Spirit of God took control of that man, and the Spirit of God went into that guy's brain and pulled out of that brain the words that were in his own vocabulary and out of his own experience and arranged them in the order that He wanted them written, the very words selected by the Holy Spirit, but selected from the life and personality of Paul so that they reflected him; nonetheless, the words of the Spirit. This is God's Word and these are God's words.

Real Life Says . . .

Our culture finds unbelievable what we believe about the Bible! When we say the Bible is God's book, that it literally is the *words of God Himself*, they look at us like they look at people who claim to have been abducted by aliens. It is more comfortable for the world to view the Bible as the religious musings of spiritual men and women on a quest to know the divine than to accept the concept that the Bible is about God communicating to us!

But Christians believe that God is personal and wants to make His love and will known. As the writer to the Hebrews says, "In the past God spoke to our forefathers through the prophets at many times and in various ways, but in these last days he has spoken to us by his Son" (Hebrews 1:1-2). God's final communication of Himself is through His Son, the Lord Jesus Christ. His words are recorded in the four Gospels, but Jesus also commissioned His apostles to be used by the Holy Spirit to teach His truth (see John 14:25-26). The sixty-six books of the Bible have been "exhaled" by a God who has not remained silent, but wants us to know His mind, His will and Himself!

But, Lord . . .

Lord, I thank You for Your Word. And I praise You for using and guiding the human writers who recorded what You wanted said. Encourage me to listen to You through them. In Jesus' name, Amen.

To Ponder . . .

A Bible which is falling apart usually belongs to someone who isn't! (Anonymous)

That's My Version and I'm Stickin' to It!

There are many different translations, paraphrases and versions of the Bible. In the study of doctrine one should use one or several reliable translations (or versions) of the Scriptures in order to understand the passage being studied.

The word may be regarded as the body of the thought, giving the spirit visibility and form. Therefore if the word is blurred, the thought is blurred, and all becomes foggy and indistinct.

(Erich Sauer)

Any man who has sense as well as faith is bound to conclude that it is the *truths* which are inspired and not the words which are merely the vehicles of truth.

(J.B. Phillips)

Every word of God is flawless. . . .
Do not add to his words,
  or he will rebuke you and prove you a liar.

(Proverbs 30:5-6)

The Knowledge Nugget

There are two extremes to be avoided by Christians today when it comes to the issue of Bible translations, versions and paraphrases.

But before we deal with those two extremes, let's define a few terms. The terms "version" and "translation" are often used synonymously to refer to the rendering of the Bible from one language into another. The Bible was not originally given in English. (Of course you knew that!) The Old Testament was written mostly in Hebrew (there are some Aramaic sections in the book of Daniel), and the New Testament was written exclusively in Greek, specifically the nonclassical Greek of the common man (called *koiné, a term meaning "common"*).

Two hundred years ago some children in the U.S. were taught Hebrew, Greek and even Latin in school and could do their own translation work in the Scriptures! Most Christians do not have the opportunity to study any of those languages, so they must find English translations or versions which are faithful to the Hebrew and Greek manuscripts which lie behind our English Bibles. Some of the more popular English Bibles in use today include the King James Version, the New International Version, the New American Standard and the New Living Translation.

The term "paraphrase" generally refers to the rendering of the Bible in one language to a different form in that same language. For example, the story behind the most successful paraphrase in history, *The Living Bible*, is that its author, Ken Taylor, wanted to make the Bible understandable to his children. As he took the subway to work each day in Chicago, he began putting the Scriptures into his own words. Although helpful, *The Living Bible* is not the best choice for a serious study Bible.

Real Life Says . . .

This discussion of what Bible one ought to use makes little sense to a world which ignores God's revelation to man. It seems little more than a kind of childish squabble among Christians. However, there are at least two extremes which must be avoided by the Christian.

One extreme is represented by those who say that there is only one translation or version of the Bible which is the Word of God. All others, they say, are either inferior or are tools of Satan to steer us away from the atoning work of Christ, His virgin birth or His deity. There are many Christians who feel that the King James Bible alone is the Word of God and any efforts to produce more "modern" translations are foolish at best and diabolical at worst.

The other extreme to avoid is represented by those who show no discernment in the version or translation they use. Certain versions are poorly done; some are mere propaganda vehicles for various cults. (*The New World Translation* of the Jehovah's Witnesses is a case in point.)

The translators of the New English Bible, for example, showed poor judgment in translating Psalm 22:16 as "they *hacked off* my hands and my feet." While the Hebrew verb in Psalm 22:16 has a variety of meanings, including *pierce, bore* and *hack off*, nearly every other translation uses the word *pierced*, which shows that the psalmist was foretelling Jesus' crucifixion. The translators of the New English Bible, however, purposely chose a meaning which obscures the prophetic significance of this Messianic Psalm. Wisdom is needed in choosing a translation of the Bible to use for serious study.

But, Lord . . .

Father, give me discernment in studying Your Word. And give me wisdom not to fight with other believers over the issue of what translation of the Scriptures we choose to use. In Jesus' name, Amen.

To Ponder . . .

Strange—the more the Bible is translated, the less it is read. (C.S. Lewis)

"For the Bible Scares Me So!"

Today's Focus

The study of the Bible for oneself need not be either a mysterious or a scary endeavor. Digging deeply into the Word of God will help one grow strong in the Christian faith.

If you want to grow in the Word of God, become a person with a chisel and quarry the Word—look, explore, seek. Let the Word become your Word, and you will grow.

(Max Lucado)

Many people think that research is a supernatural gift of the gods. It is simply an idea from a troubled mind, an inspiration followed by infinitely painstaking work and perspiration.

(Sir Frederick Banting)

Study to shew thyself approved unto God, a workman that needeth not to be ashamed, rightly dividing the word of truth.

(2 Timothy 2:15, KJV)

The Knowledge Nugget

When our son was four or five, he would go around the house singing, "Jesus loves me, this I know, for the Bible *scares* me so. . . ." We didn't teach him to sing those words, but they do seem to express the fear that many Christians have of studying the Word of God. But the treasures of the very truths of God await those believers who dare to dive into the Bible for themselves.

In the King James Version of the Bible, Second Timothy 2:15 says, "Study to shew thyself approved unto God, a workman that needeth not to be ashamed, rightly dividing the word of truth." The word "study" really means "be diligent." To "divide the word of truth" really means to interpret the Word correctly. The believer in Christ is to be diligent in committing himself to being a laborer in the Word of God, so that he will not be ashamed. Many followers of Christ don't know what the Word says, much less what it *means*. It appears that for a lot of Christians the theme-verse of their lives is not Second Timothy 2:15, but rather Ecclesiastes 12:12: "Of making many books there is no end, and much study wearies the body."

I don't know many Christians who have become *weary* from studying the Bible, do you? Instead, we are often like the bears I mentioned in Section One, Day 25. Apparently every year after the tourist season is over and the snow falls, dozens of bears die by the side of the road. The reason, park rangers say, is that the bears are still waiting for handouts from the tourists. They have become dependent upon *others* to provide their meals, which has short-circuited their natural instinct to forage for their own food! How sad.

Real Life Says . . .

Many people are indeed afraid of the Bible, although they may not admit it. Perhaps they have never been given any good reasons for believing the Bible to be from the true God. Perhaps they are following another "holy" book (remember our discussion on the canon on Day 12?) and need to be shown that the Bible and the Bible alone is the Word of God. Perhaps they realize that if the Bible is the Word of God, then they are in a lot of trouble. Most would prefer to stay away from even the possibility of an authoritative, inerrant communication from the real God. And they would never consider opening up a Gideon Bible in a hotel room, lest God sneak up on them and invade their lives! One is reminded of Jeremiah's statement: "The word of the LORD is offensive to them; they find no pleasure in it" (Jeremiah 6:10).

The reality is that the Bible *is* the Word of God and it stands waiting for the diligent study of the Christian. A Dade County, Florida public school-system pamphlet announced: "Homework will be assigned during the entire school year as *doomed* necessary by the teachers." For many Christians that pretty much sums up their view of the study of the Bible.

But, Lord . . .

Father, forgive me when I am afraid of Your Word. Cause it to become the joy and rejoicing of my heart. And help me to model to others a longing to dig deep into Your truth. In Jesus' name, Amen.

To Ponder . . .

Every day, study serves to show how much I have yet to learn upon those subjects of which it is my duty to know everything. Give me time. (Robert Sauthy)

"Go, and Do Thou Likewise!"

If the Christian recognizes the Bible as the source of God's truth and commits himself to delving deeply into that Word, then he must be careful not to take verses out of context.

Let him who does wrong continue to do wrong; let him who is vile continue to be vile.

(Revelation 22:11)

. . . Christ has not been raised . . .

(1 Corinthians 15:14)

A feast is made for laughter,
 and wine makes life merry,
 but money is the answer for everything.

(Ecclesiastes 10:19)

The Knowledge Nugget

When I was a seminary student, the wife of one of my favorite profs was a gifted speaker for women's conferences and retreats. She tells about one mother-daughter banquet to which she was invited and was asked to serve as their main speaker. The theme for the banquet was decided, a large banner was ordered for the meeting room, and she was asked to speak on the theme, "Like Mother, Like Daughter," from Ezekiel 16:44. The only problem was the *context* of that verse. The context has to do with the sin of prostitution!

It is relatively easy to find a phrase which strikes us and to ignore the surrounding verses (the immediate context) or the purpose of the book in which it is found (the wider context). When Solomon says in Ecclesiastes 10:19, "A feast is made for laughter, and wine makes life merry, but money is the answer for everything," he is speaking from the perspective of life without God, life lived only "under the sun."

Our tendency to take verses out of context comes from lazy Bible study methods. Some Christians treat the Word of God almost like a daily horoscope, opening the Bible at random and picking out a verse for the day. I heard of one young man who felt this was the way to get daily guidance from God. So on Monday he opened his Bible randomly and dropped his finger down on Ecclesiastes 9:10, which reads, "Whatever your hand finds to do, do it with all your might." He wasn't sure what that meant, but couldn't wait to see what verse God would "give" him the next day. On Tuesday he opened his Bible with anticipation. As he allowed his Bible to drop open, his finger landed on Luke 10:37, where Jesus says, "Go and do likewise." With even greater anticipation, on Wednesday he opened his Bible and dropped his finger down on Matthew 27:5, which reads, "Then [Judas] went away and hanged himself"!

That is hardly good Bible study! If we are to grow deep in the things of God, then we need to study verses in their context, recognize which verses have primary application to us and be careful in the way we connect various passages of Scripture to each other.

Real Life Says . . .

Our world does not accept the Bible as the Word of God, so it shows little concern for the problem of taking verses out of context. For us believers it is a serious matter that we not "twist" the Scriptures to suit our understanding, but allow each passage to make its own point.

In the area of theology, I know of one scholar who has misused Psalm 139. David said, "Where can I go from your Spirit? Where can I flee from your presence? . . . If I make my bed in the depths [of hell], you are there" (139:7-8). This theologian says that the Lord is present in hell. And if He is present in hell as Creator, perhaps He is present in hell as Redeemer. Therefore, he suggests, those who go to hell may have hope one day of being freed and being translated to heaven!

But the Bible offers no such hope to the lost. Taking verses out of context and using them to deny the clear teaching of other sections of the Bible is not Bible study!

But, Lord . . .

Father, it is sometimes difficult to take the time to study Your Word properly. I certainly don't want to misrepresent Your truth. Help me by Your Spirit to do the work I need to do. In Jesus' name, Amen.

To Ponder . . .

There is an old saying which proclaims, "A text without a context is a pretext."

The Joy of Unit-Reading

To "unit-read" a book of the Bible means to read an entire book through at one sitting. This approach to many of the books of the Bible will prove useful in understanding overall themes.

The greatest gift is the passion for reading. It is cheap, it consoles, it distracts, it excites, it gives you knowledge of the world and experience of a wide kind. It is a moral illumination.

(Elizabeth Hardwick)

Bury yourself in good books; develop a thirst for printer's ink and quench it by reading, for from books flows the fountain of youth found by few.

(Larry T. McGeHee)

When your words came, I ate them;
   they were my joy and my heart's delight,
for I bear your name,
   O LORD God Almighty.

(Jeremiah 15:16)

The Knowledge Nugget

In an earlier devotional we emphasized the importance of the discipline of reading. There we referred to the powerful question by Herrick Johnson who asked, "If God is a reality, and the soul is a reality, and you are an immortal being, what are you doing with your Bible shut?"

Christians may not have their Bibles completely shut, but often they are open for only a few minutes at a time! Many of us read only snippets of Scripture—a verse here, a psalm there—failing to invest the quality time necessary to understand whole books of the Bible.

Mark Twain defined a "classic" as "a book everybody has, but no one reads." The Bible is composed of *sixty-six* classics that few Christians ever sit down and read straight through. Part of the problem, of course, is that we have become accustomed to the chapter and verse divisions in our Bibles and assume that they are almost the equivalent of stop signs! By the way, the chapter and verse divisions are not inspired by God but were developed over a thousand years after the close of the biblical canon!

University professor William J. Bennett tells his students that although he is teaching them an introductory philosophy course, he is really seeking to give them a course in slow reading. He says that many of his students are the happy graduates of speed-reading courses. But his purpose is to get them to slow down, to cherish the language used by the writer. "Possibly by the end of the course," Bennett says, "they will read fifty words a minute, with a text that deserves to be read that slowly."

The Word of God, the Bible, deserves to be read slowly. And it deserves to be read as individual books. When we speak of "unit-reading," we are not suggesting that every book of the Bible ought to be read at one sitting, but many of them should. The book of Psalms does not appear to be written to be read at one time, but what about the book of Isaiah, or Ezekiel, or Mark's Gospel? One of the primary features of Mark's Gospel—the immediacy of Jesus' acts of service, portraying Him as the Perfect Servant—will most likely not be seen *unless* one unit-reads it!

Real Life Says . . .

To read straight through a religious book makes little sense to many in our culture. They would not hesitate to spend six hours pouring over a popular mystery novel or three hours watching a baseball game. But the thought of dedicating oneself to grasping the overall theme of Daniel, or seeing the structure of the seven miracles of Jesus in John's Gospel, has no appeal to them. But it ought to have an appeal to us!

Jeremiah says, "When your words came, I ate them; they were my joy and my heart's delight, for I bear your name, O LORD God Almighty" (Jeremiah 15:16). Many Christians, if they were honest, would have to rephrase that verse to read, "When your words came, we were too busy to read them," or, "We are on a spiritual diet!" or, "Thanks, Lord, but we would prefer to just take small bites of Your truth." Junk food can easily be substituted for good food!

But, Lord . . .

Father, I thank You for the banquet of Your Word. Help me to feast on Your truth! In Jesus' name, Amen.

To Ponder . . .

Don't just nibble at God's Word—feast!

The Bible Jesus Read—Part 1

For various reasons Christians often ignore seventy-five percent of the Word of God, namely the Old Testament, the sole authority for the Lord Jesus, the apostles and the early Church. Much of the New Testament makes little sense without understanding its Old Testament background.

The early church was quite right to keep the Old Testament in the beginning, but she should have jettisoned it very soon. It was a disaster for the Lutheran reform to keep it in the 16th century. But for Protestantism to cling to it as a canonical document in the 20th century is a sign of religious and ecclesial [church] paralysis.

(Adolph Harnack)

In our time, says one church historian, the social liberals have sought to recover the Gospels, the Pentecostals the book of Acts, and the evangelicals the Epistles. Perhaps we should join together ecumenically to recover the biblical books that preceded all of those.

(Philip Yancey)

I remember your ancient laws, O LORD,
   and I find comfort in them.

(Psalm 119:52)

DAY TWENTY .... *The Absolute Need for an Absolute Authority*

The Knowledge Nugget

In his landmark book, *The Bible Jesus Read*, Philip Yancey states that, according to recent polls, eighty percent of Americans claim to believe in the Ten Commandments, but very few can name as many as four of them. One-half of all adult Americans are unable to identify the Bible's first book as Genesis. And fourteen percent identify Joan of Arc as Noah's wife!

We are probably not surprised at the biblical illiteracy of the world, but how much of the Old Testament do evangelical Christians know? And some believers act as if the New Testament has replaced the Old, that the New Testament is more "inspired." (Perhaps our red-letter editions of the New Testament which highlight the words of Jesus have contributed to this thinking.) When Paul writes to Timothy that "All Scripture is God-breathed and is useful for teaching, rebuking, correcting and training in righteousness, so that the man of God may be thoroughly equipped for every good work" (2 Timothy 3:16-17), he is referring to the Old Testament!

Real Life Says . . .

Many today consider both the Old and New Testaments only ancient graffiti. But evangelical Christianity teaches that *all sixty-six books of the Bible* are out-breathed by God. However, the lion's share of the Christian's time in the Word of God is probably not spent in the thirty-nine books of the Old Testament. In fact, it seems to me that Christians spend most of their time in the Gospel of John and the Epistles of Paul.

A hundred years ago the liberal church historian Adolph Harnack suggested that the Old Testament should have been "jettisoned" long ago (see full quote above). It seems that many Christians have actually followed Harnack's advice, for the Old Testament is frequently studied only in Sunday school.

Although most Christians believe in the principle known as "progressive revelation" (which means that God did not tell us all we needed to know in the Old Testament, but gradually communicated His full truth through all sixty-six books of the entire Bible), that does *not* mean that the Old Testament is inferior to the New Testament, or that it is no longer of any "use" to the Christian, or that it has been "superceded" by the New. Yancey is right when he says that neither Testament is enough. We need both Testaments in order to know the mind and will of God.

The psalmist says, "I remember your ancient laws, O LORD, and I find comfort in them" (Psalm 119:52). Today's evangelical Christians need to repent of their virtual acceptance of Harnack's abominable advice! We must return to the *entire* Word of God.

But, Lord . . .

Father, thank You for the fullness of Your Word. Help me to be like my Savior and revere Your complete revelation to me. In Jesus' name, Amen.

To Ponder . . .

Today we need an "Emmaus road" experience in reverse. The disciples knew Moses and the Prophets but could not conceive how they might relate to Jesus the Christ. The modern Church knows Jesus the Christ but is fast losing any grasp of Moses and the Prophets. (Philip Yancey)

The Bible Jesus Read—Part 2

The serious Christian needs to dedicate time and energy to uncovering what can be learned about God's love and His will from the Old Testament.

There is one sentence all humankind craves to hear: "The Maker of all things loves and wants me."

(Reynolds Price)

Job convinces me that God cares more about our faith than our pleasure.

(Philip Yancey)

You diligently study the Scriptures because you think that by them you possess eternal life. These are the Scriptures that testify about me, yet you refuse to come to me to have life.

(John 5:39-40)

The Knowledge Nugget

We saw in yesterday's devotional that many Christians miss seventy-five percent of God's Word because they ignore the Old Testament Scriptures. Some are convinced that the New Testament has replaced the Old, and therefore the Old is no longer needed. Others have misunderstood the purpose of some versions putting the words of the Lord Jesus in red type. As a friend of mine says, "*All* the Bible is of 'red-letter' authority!" We would not suggest that the things which were written by the Apostle Paul or the Apostle John are not God's Word because they are not in red type, would we?

Still others may think that because much of the Old Testament is narrative (story) in form, its primary use is as Sunday school material for our children. But I agree with the preacher who said that the Old Testament stories are *way too good* to be confined to our Sunday school handouts and flannelgraph boards! In fact, if one studies the stories of the Old Testament (episodes like Daniel in the lions' den, or David killing Goliath, or Balaam having a long conversation with his donkey), one finds powerful theological points being made in each event. It may be an indication that we have lost the value of *stories* in our virtual abandonment of the Old Testament scriptures.

G.K. Chesterton said, "The central idea of the great part of the Old Testament may be called the idea of the loneliness of God." His loneliness, His longing to make a people for His very own, is chronicled throughout the pages of the thirty-nine books of the Old Testament. From the call of Abram in Genesis 12 to Hosea's lament over his adulterous wife, God cries out that He wants a love relationship with His people—and will spare nothing to achieve that. In fact, the entire Old Testament points clearly to the sending of the "suffering Servant of Jehovah" (Isaiah 42–53), the One who would come in order to bear the sins of the world. God, as it were, wears His heart on His sleeve, when He has Ezekiel write,

> Rid yourselves of all the offenses you have committed, and get a new heart and a new spirit. Why will you die, O house of Israel? For I take no pleasure in the death of anyone, declares the Sovereign LORD. Repent and live! (Ezekiel 18:31-32)

Real Life Says . . .

Our culture seems clueless about God's pursuit of a people for His name. Peter uses language of the minor prophet Hosea to remind his readers,

> You are a chosen people, a royal priesthood, a holy nation, a people belonging to God, that you may declare the praises of him who called you out of darkness into his wonderful light. Once you were not a people, but now you are the people of God; once you had not received mercy, but now you have received mercy. (1 Peter 2:9-10)

The Old Testament reverberates with God's voice calling out to sinners to repent and be forgiven. And it details God's plan to accomplish salvation on a righteous basis. The New Testament, of course, is God's plan coming to completion in the giving of God's Son, the Lord Jesus Christ. As the Apostle Paul writes, "He who did not spare his own Son, but gave him up for us all—how will he not also, along with him, graciously give us all things?" (Romans 8:32).

But, Lord . . .

Father, I repent of my sometimes low view of the first half of Your precious Word. Thank You for Your loving pursuit of a people for Your name. Help me to tell the whole story of that provision of Your Son, as revealed in all of Your Word. In Jesus' name, Amen.

To Ponder . . .

"See, I have engraved you on the palms of my hands." (Isaiah 49:16)

A Divine Bible Study—Part 1

It is possible to read the Old Testament and miss the truths about Christ. This happened to His disciples and it happened to the religious leaders of Israel. The answer, however, is not to allegorize all the verses of the Old Testament (that is, to make them appear to be speaking directly about Christ when they aren't), but to understand the themes of Scripture which culminate in Christ.

The things in the Bible I don't understand don't bother me! It's the things in the Bible I *do* understand—those things bother me!

(Mark Twain)

What makes the difference is not how many times you have been through the Bible, but how many times and how thoroughly the Bible has been through you.

(Gipsy Smith)

Were not our hearts burning within us while he talked with us on the road and opened the Scriptures to us?

(Luke 24:32)

The Knowledge Nugget

Chuck Matlock, a Michigan elementary school teacher, was so convinced that his school's students couldn't read 7,000 books during March (which is National Reading Month) that he said he'd eat worms if they did. He lost the bet. The 232 students read 7,785 volumes in that month. So Matlock boiled four worms in lemon juice and salt and downed them before the students. Ever the teacher, Matlock said to the children, "Really, worms have as much protein as a T-bone steak without the gristle." He added that he's game for a similar challenge next year!

One wonders what it will take on the part of pastors to get their *congregations* reading! John Calvin, the great Reformer, declared, "Unless God's Word illumine the way, the whole life of men is wrapped in darkness and mist, so that they cannot but miserably stray." Simply reading the Word of God is not enough. We must *understand* what we are reading.

In Luke 24 we have the wonderful story of two disciples walking to the village of Emmaus in great despair because their Messiah and friend, Jesus of Nazareth, had just been crucified. The resurrected Jesus Himself meets them on the road and they do not recognize Him. Jesus feigns ignorance and asks them what they are discussing as they are walking (24:17). Cleopas, the only one named of the two, seems to respond in anger and says, "Are you only a visitor to Jerusalem and do not know the things that have happened there in these days?" (24:18). The ironic point, of course, is that those "things" have been happening to *Jesus*!

He responds, "What things?" (24:19) giving Cleopas and his friend an opportunity to pour out their broken hearts to this "stranger."

"Well, the things about Jesus of Nazareth!" says Cleopas. "He was a prophet, powerful in word and deed before God and all the people. The chief priests and our rulers handed him over to be sentenced to death, and they crucified him; but we had hoped that he was the one who was going to redeem Israel. And what is more, it is the third day since all this took place" (24:19-21).

This disciple continues to dump on the stranger. To paraphrase a bit, he says, "And we are also having trouble with our women. Some went to Jesus' tomb and claim that His body was gone. They even said they had a vision of angels who said that Jesus was alive. Women are so unreliable, you know?" But then he reluctantly adds, "Then some of our companions went to the tomb and found it just as the women had said, but him they did not see" (24:24). How hard it is for a man to say to a woman, "You were r-r-r-r-right!"

Real Life Says . . .

Our society mocks the idea of a dead man becoming alive again. And that appears to have been Cleopas and his friend's problem as well. The bodily resurrection of Jesus of Nazareth should not have taken them by surprise. As we will see in tomorrow's devotional, the presence of unbelief, specifically failing to see the Old Testament's testimony to Christ, was their problem.

But, Lord . . .

Father, it is so easy for me to judge Cleopas and his friend for not believing the prophecies of the Old Testament and the promises of Your Son. Help me to see that I probably would have been just as foolish and unbelieving. In Jesus' name, Amen.

To Ponder . . .

Got a broken heart? Jesus is listening!

A Divine Bible Study—Part 2

Factors such as our own foolishness and slowness of heart can keep us from understanding Scripture's central theme: the person and work of the Lord Jesus Christ.

When the president of the American Bible Society was asked how to keep a leather-bound Bible from stiffening and cracking, he said: "There is one oil that is especially good for the treatment of leather on Bibles. In fact, it will ensure that your Bible will stay in good condition. It is not sold, but you can find it in the palm of the human hand."

If when I get to heaven the Lord shall say to me, "Spurgeon, I want you to preach for all eternity," I would reply, "Lord, give me a Bible, that is all I need."

(C.H. Spurgeon)

And beginning with Moses and all the Prophets, he explained to them what was said in all the Scriptures concerning himself. . . . Then he opened their minds so they could understand the Scriptures.

(Luke 24:27, 45)

The Knowledge Nugget

As we saw in yesterday's devotional, the two disciples on the road to Emmaus were joined by a stranger who was none other than the resurrected Lord Jesus. They did not know it was He, and they unburden their hearts about their friend having been executed. Their own unbelief had missed what the Old Testament prophecies said.

The irony in Luke 24 is almost humorous. The risen Lord is walking with these two distraught disciples, having fulfilled His promise that He would conquer death and the grave, yet they are freely expressing their despair that Jesus has been crucified. In fact, one of them says, "And what is more, it is the *third day* since all this took place" (24:21, emphasis added). What meaning would the expression "the third day" have to a total stranger? None. But to *Jesus and His disciples* it was a reminder that He had promised on numerous occasions *to rise from the dead the third day* (Matthew 16:21; 17:23; 20:19; 27:63). Jesus had kept His word, but these two disciples did not recognize that fact. Yet.

They refused to believe the testimony of the women who had seen the empty tomb. And this "stranger" rebukes them by saying, "How foolish you are, and how slow of heart to believe all that the prophets have spoken! Did not the Christ have to suffer these things and then enter his glory?" (Luke 24:25-26). He then led them in a divine Bible study: "And beginning with Moses and all the Prophets, he explained to them what was said in all the Scriptures concerning himself" (24:27). He rebukes their "foolishness" because it is *foolish* to mourn a dead Savior who has risen from the dead! Such wasted anguish makes no sense when God is as good as His Word!

They also suffered from slowness of heart. I have a friend who sometimes experiences a rapid heart rate. His heart begins to palpitate at an increased rate, which can be dangerous. Have you ever considered the fact that a heart that is too "slow" may also be dangerous? A hesitancy to believe God's truth can lead to a slow heart.

Real Life Says . . .

Our world doesn't know what to do with this passage. Viewing the Bible as something less than the Word of God and the resurrection of Jesus as wishful thinking, the world misses the point: Jesus Christ is the culmination of the Father's desire to provide salvation for all who believe. And even death itself cannot stand in the way of the Father's plan! But *unbelief* can keep one from experiencing the transforming power of that victory!

The disciples recognize that this Bible study leader is none other than Jesus Himself when He goes home with them and eats with them. Perhaps they saw the nail prints in His wrists; perhaps there was something unique about the way He broke the matzoh (bread); perhaps it was simply that God unveiled their eyes. But their response of faith should be ours: "Were not our hearts burning within us while he talked with us on the road and opened the Scriptures to us?" (24:32).

But, Lord . . .

Father, please give me a heart which beats rapidly not only to believe Your Word but also to do what Your Word says. In Jesus' name, Amen.

To Ponder . . .

Does your heart beat fast when it is around the Word of God?

To Err Is Human?

The doctrine of inerrancy states that the original manuscripts of the Bible did not contain any errors and that such perfection extends to our translations today to the degree that they are faithful to those manuscripts.

The status of the Bible is one of sufficiency rather than of perfection.

(James Barr)

Sometimes I think Paul is wrong and I have ventured to say so.

(C.H. Dodd)

I have spoken to you of earthly things and you do not believe; how then will you believe if I speak of heavenly things?

(John 3:12)

The Knowledge Nugget

If the Bible is the Word of God and our primary source for our theology, then it matters greatly whether or not we can trust the content of that book. Do we stand in judgment of it—or does it stand in judgment of us? The doctrine of inerrancy argues that a fully trustworthy God used error-prone, fallen human authors to communicate His mind and will to us without mistake. Just as the Holy Spirit "over-shadowed" the virgin Mary so that "the holy one to be born [would] be called the Son of God" (Luke 1:35), so evangelical Christians believe that the Holy Spirit overshadowed (theologians use the term "superintended") the human writers of Scripture so that what they wrote was indeed the very Word of God.

Christians work hard at seeking to reconcile what the Bible says with what science proclaims. But why all the fuss? Sir Winston Churchill in *My Early Life* wrote:

> I have always been surprised to see some of our bishops and clergy making such heavy weather about reconciling the Bible story with modern scientific and historical knowledge. Why do they want to reconcile them? If you are the recipient of a message which cheers your heart and fortifies your soul, which promises you reunion with those you have loved in a world of larger opportunity and wider sympathies, why should you worry about the shape or color of the travel-stained envelope; whether it is duly stamped, whether the date on the postmark is right or wrong? These matters may be puzzling, but they are certainly not important. What is important is the message and the benefits to you of receiving it.

Real Life Says . . .

"Righto, old chap!" says the world to Churchill's opinion. Is the Christian who seeks to defend the doctrine of inerrancy simply "making heavy weather"? Are the only central issues the importance of the message and whether or not I am receiving its benefits?

Of course the message is the main thing. And if I am not believing and receiving that message, it makes little sense to argue for the perfection of that message within the pages of an ancient book. But the idea that one may divorce the spiritual message of the Bible from its historical or geographical or scientific details and framework is exceedingly dangerous.

Jesus said in John 3: "I have spoken to you [plural] of earthly things and you [plural] do not believe; how then will you [plural] believe if I speak of heavenly things?" (3:12). Although this passage records Jesus' conversation with one individual (Nicodemus, a leader of the Pharisees), the Greek language makes it perfectly clear that He is addressing more than Nicodemus. This religious leader had come to Jesus individually, but he had begun the conversation by stating, "*We* know you are a teacher who has come from God" (3:2, emphasis added). Jesus then speaks to Nicodemus both as an individual ("Do not marvel that I said to *you* . . .", [3:7]) and as a representative of Israel's religion ("*You* [plural] must be born again!", [3:7, NKJV]).

Jesus then shifts to only the plural "you" in the following verses, including our verse: "If you [plural] do not believe when I speak of earthly things, how will you [plural] believe if I speak of heavenly things?" (3:12, author paraphrase).

The point of this devotional is that Jesus is to be trusted in both earthly and heavenly matters. Similarly, Jesus' *word* is to be trusted in both earthly and heavenly matters. That is not to say that the Bible is a mathematics textbook, but where it speaks of science or geography or history, it is trustworthy.

But, Lord . . .

Father, thank You for Your inerrant Word. Help me to believe it today. In Jesus' name, Amen.

To Ponder . . .

Inerrancy affirms that the Bible is nothing less than revelation, revelation that comes to us from a transcendent, personal God. (R.C. Sproul)

On a Wing and a . . .

Today's Focus

Bible study without prayer can lead to empty orthodoxy or cold intellectualism. Prayer without Bible study can be uninformed and immature emotionalism. The Christian who wants to grow deep in the truths of the Christian faith needs both serious study of the Word and dependent prayer for the illuminating ministry of the Holy Spirit.

If you have the Bible alone, you will dry up. If you have the Spirit alone, you will blow up. If you have the Bible and the Spirit, you will grow up!

(Anonymous)

Prayer is not a monologue, but a dialogue. Listening to God's voice is the secret of the assurance that He will listen to mine.

(Andrew Murray)

I pray also that the eyes of your heart may be enlightened in order that you may know the hope to which he has called you, the riches of his glorious inheritance in the saints, and his incomparably great power for us who believe.

(Ephesians 1:18-19)

The Knowledge Nugget

I once heard a preacher ask, "What is more important: your listening to God or God's listening to you?" The "right" answer, as far as he was concerned, was that it is *far* more important to listen to God speaking to us in His Word than for us to speak to God through prayer. I don't like the way that question was worded. It seems to me that it is like asking, "What is more important: inhaling or exhaling?" The answer, of course, is that both are important!

When asked a similar question, the great spiritual writer and pastor A.W. Tozer replied, "Which is more important to a bird: the right wing or the left?" We need both serious study of the Word of God and dependent prayer for the Holy Spirit to open our minds and move our wills to become the people God wants us to be.

There are liberal theologians who have studied the Bible for years, but they remain outside the family of God. How is it that they have missed the gospel, the good news, about Jesus Christ? The doctrine of the illumination of the Spirit appears to be the explanation.

Real Life Says . . .

Those who study the Bible merely as literature may learn great content and miss the great King. This happened to the Jewish leaders who eventually rejected Jesus. Jesus said to them, "You diligently study the Scriptures because you think that by them you possess eternal life. These are the Scriptures that testify about me, yet you refuse to come to me to have life" (John 5:39-40). Because they studied Scripture for the wrong reason, they missed the major point of the Old Testament prophecies: a suffering Savior who would die for His people's sins.

Jesus referred to the illuminating ministry of the Spirit of God when He promised to send this divine substitute teacher: "The Counselor, the Holy Spirit, whom the Father will send in my name, will teach you all things and will remind you of everything I have said to you" (14:26). Obviously this Spirit would guide the apostles in their writing of Holy Scripture (what we call the New Testament), but the general teaching ministry of the Spirit to all believers seems to be implied. In the next chapter Jesus added, "When the Counselor comes, whom I will send to you from the Father, the Spirit of truth who goes out from the Father, he will testify about me" (15:26).

The Apostle Paul prayed for the Ephesian believers "that the eyes of your heart may be enlightened in order that you may know the hope to which he has called you, the riches of his glorious inheritance in the saints, and his incomparably great power for us who believe" (Ephesians 1:18-19). The Holy Spirit is the great Enlightener—and He is just a prayer away!

But, Lord . . .

Father, I thank You for Your Word. And I praise You for Your Spirit who wants to illumine my mind and stir my emotions that I might grow in my Christian hope. Move my will, Spirit of God, that I might experience the riches of that inheritance! In Jesus' name, Amen.

To Ponder . . .

To be the light of the world the believer needs the illuminating ministry of the Spirit.

Better Than Fort Knox!

The truths of the Word of God not only will enrich our lives, but will also bring our thinking into conformity with those things that please the Lord.

Money is the number one cause of domestic unhappiness. Many couples need to undergo plastic surgery. They need to have their credit cards cut off.

(Dr. Ed Wheat)

J.P. Morgan was once asked, "How much money does it take to make a man really happy?" His answer was: "Just a little more."

The law from your mouth is more precious to me
than thousands of pieces of silver and gold.

(Psalm 119:72)

The Knowledge Nugget

Fort Knox, an American military post near Louisville, Kentucky, covers about 33,000 acres. Apart from being a training center for the armored units of the U.S. Army and a museum of World War II artifacts, Fort Knox houses the greater part of the gold reserve of the U.S. government. The steel and concrete vault beneath the fortified building rests on solid rock and is sixty feet long by forty feet wide. Its walls are over two feet thick and the vault door weighs more than twenty tons. No one person is entrusted with the combination. The outer wall of the depository is constructed of granite lined with concrete. Construction materials used on the building include 16,500 cubic feet of granite, 4,200 cubic yards of concrete, 750 tons of reinforcing steel and 670 tons of structural steel. The gold stored in Fort Knox is in the form of bars (somewhat smaller than an ordinary building brick), each weighing about twenty-seven pounds and worth about $17,000. The report is that $6 billion in gold is housed at Fort Knox.

Several times in Scripture the expression "silver and gold" is used. For example, Peter writes:

> For you know that it was not with perishable things such as silver or gold that you were redeemed from the empty way of life handed down to you from your forefathers, but with the precious blood of Christ, a lamb without blemish or defect. . . . For you have been born again, not of perishable seed, but of imperishable, through the living and enduring word of God" (1 Peter 1:18-19, 23).

"Silver or gold" are referred to here as perishable. Our salvation was not purchased by something perishable. The precious, unblemished blood of Christ was the imperishable means used by God to purchase our redemption.

The writer of Proverbs speaks of the fear of the Lord as something to be more earnestly sought than silver:

> My son, if you accept my words
>   and store up my commands within you,
> turning your ear to wisdom
>   and applying your heart to understanding,
> and if you call out for insight
>   and cry aloud for understanding,
> and if you look for it as for silver
>   and search for it as for hidden treasure,

then you will understand the fear of the LORD
and find the knowledge of God. (Proverbs 2:1-5)

Real Life Says . . .

Many in our world have no idea what a gift we possess in the Bible, the Word of God. They either place it on the level of other human, religious books which might occasionally inspire, or they treat it as part of the paraphernalia of pious people. But it is a treasure which brings eternal reward.

In 1996 the *Chicago Tribune* ran the story of Buddy Post, described as "living proof that money can't buy happiness." After winning $16.2 million in the 1988 Pennsylvania lottery, he was convicted of assault, left by his sixth wife, almost killed by his brother and successfully sued by his landlady for one-third of the jackpot. "Money didn't change me," said Post, a fifty-eight-year-old former carnival worker and cook. "It changed people around me that I knew, that I thought cared a little bit about me. But they only cared about the money." Post is trying to auction off seventeen future payments, valued at nearly $5 million, in order to pay off taxes, legal fees and a number of failed business ventures. "Money draws flies," he says. Pursuing the truths of the Word of God is far better than winning the lottery or getting all the gold in Fort Knox!

But, Lord . . .

Father, sometimes my values are so mixed-up. Help me to value Your Word and to be thankful for the riches that it brings. In Jesus' name, Amen.

To Ponder . . .

Can you honestly say that God's Word is precious to you?

Sometimes Dry as a Stick!

When the study of the Word of God becomes boring, keeping certain truths in mind can help the believer move ahead in maturity and not become discouraged by the Evil One.

I have sometimes seen more in a line of the Bible than I could well tell how to stand under, and yet at another time the whole Bible hath been to me as dry as a stick.

(John Bunyan)

Surely it must be a sin to bore God's people with God's Word!

(Daryl Busby)

Open my eyes that I may see
   wonderful things in your law.

(Psalm 119:18)

The Knowledge Nugget

How can the believer in Christ maintain his enthusiasm for getting into the Word of God? Boredom, like enthusiasm, is contagious, and many Christians mistakenly expect the life of faith to be a continuous series of exciting experiences. It is not surprising that when times of spiritual dryness come, those believers are thrown for a loop!

The Absolute Need for an Absolute Authority .... DAY TWENTY-SEVEN

The Screwtape Letters by C.S. Lewis is a collection of fictional correspondence between an arch-demon Screwtape and his nephew understudy demon, Wormwood, about how to trip up human beings. One letter from Screwtape has to do with what Lewis calls the law of "undulation," which refers to the alternating spiritual highs and lows of the believer who is seriously following God. How is the believer to deal with periods of dryness? Screwtape advises Wormwood, "Let him [the Christian Wormwood is tempting] assume that the first ardours of his conversion might have been expected to last, and ought to have lasted, forever, and that his present dryness is an equally permanent condition." The demons want to discourage the believer and so they seek to maximize the periods of dryness, focus his attention on his lack of joy or enthusiasm or cause him to think that he is just going through a "phase" (by embracing the Christian faith). They want the Christian to become discouraged and take his mind off the truths of God.

My mother (who is now with the Lord in heaven) used to say, "I steadfastly refuse to gratify the devil by being discouraged!" Discouragement is one of Satan's most powerful tools, and he can even wield it against the believer who wants to study the Word of God.

Real Life Says . . .

Our world tries to brainwash us into thinking that the most important thing in life is our own happiness, and that if our experiences do not bring us to a certain level of happiness, we need to move on to something else. But happiness was never intended to be pursued as an end in itself. In fact, happiness is a by-product of *holiness*. And how does the believer become holy? Well, that precise question is asked by the psalmist: "How can a young man keep his way pure? *By living according to your word*" (Psalm 119:9, emphasis added). As we saw in our other devotionals on Psalm 119 (Days 8-10 in this section), the Word of God promises many riches to the one who pursues God through His Word.

Our archenemy Satan wants to derail that pursuit! And if he can do that by causing us to quit the study of the Word because it sometimes becomes "as dry as a stick," then that technique will be used by him to the fullest.

How can we move out of that "dry as a stick" discouragement? The psalmist gives us the answer in the verses following the question of how a young man can keep his way pure: "I seek you with all my heart; do not let me stray from your commands. I have hidden your word in my heart that I might not sin against you" (119:10-11).

But, Lord . . .

Father, sometimes I am such an easy prey for the Evil One! I need my eyes open every day to see the wonderful things in Your law. And I need Your Spirit to encourage me to seek You with all my heart. In Jesus' name, Amen.

To Ponder . . .

When you get serious with God, Satan gets serious with you! (Stephen Brown)

A Holy Rage

The serious study of the Word of God should not only advance the believer in a love for the lost, but also develop within the follower of Christ an anguish, a holy rage, at the destructive power of sin.

Lawyer coming home to wife: "It was a terrible day in court—I exhibited moral outrage when I meant to show righteous indignation."

H.W. Beecher says that "a man that does not know how to be angry, does not know how to be good. A man that does not know how to be shaken to his heart's core with indignation over things evil, is either a fungus, or a wicked man."

Seek good, not evil,
    that you may live.
Then the LORD God Almighty will be with you,
    just as you say he is.
Hate evil, love good;
    maintain justice in the courts.

(Amos 5:14-15)

The Knowledge Nugget

One of the greatest misconceptions of the world around us is the idea that Christianity makes people *nice—ONLY nice*! The very idea that Christians should get angry or demonstrate a holy rage shocks and scandalizes some people.

Common sayings suggest that there is only one kind of anger: destructive. Someone has said, "Anger is just one letter short of danger." Another has written: "Anger is a wind which blows out the lamp of the mind."

But such sentiments do not completely square with the teaching of the Bible, the Word of God. Indeed there is unholy anger, which is soundly condemned by James: "Everyone should be quick to listen, slow to speak and slow to become angry, for man's anger does not bring about the righteous life that God desires" (James 1:19-20).

Real Life Says . . .

The world around us is puzzled about this issue of anger in the Christian. The Bible does teach the concept of *righteous* anger. (A little boy defined "righteous indignation" as "when you get angry without cussin'!") Jeremiah tells us that "The fierce anger of the LORD will not turn back until he fully accomplishes the purposes of his heart" (Jeremiah 30:24). If "it is sin not to be angry with sin" (Thomas Fuller), then we need to sit up and pay attention when the Bible says that "God is angry with the wicked every day" (Psalm 7:11, KJV). God's wrath against sin is His necessary reaction to objective moral evil. And His people should be angry at the things that anger God!

Kaj Munk, a Danish pastor who was executed by the Nazis in January of 1944, put it this way:

> What is therefore the task of the preacher today? Shall I answer "faith, hope, and love"? That sounds beautiful. But I would say *courage*. No, even that is not challenging enough to be the whole truth. Our task today is *recklessness*. For what we Christians lack is most assuredly not psychology or literature. *We lack a holy rage*. A holy rage. The recklessness that

comes from a knowledge of God and humanity. The ability to rage when justice lies prostrate on the streets and the lie rages across the face of the earth, a holy anger about things that are wrong in the world, to rage against the ravaging of God's earth and the destruction of God's world, to rage when little children must die of hunger, when the tables of the rich are sagging with food, to rage at the senseless killing of so many, and against the madness of militaries, to rage at the lie that calls the threat of death and the strategy of destruction peace, to rage against complacency, to restlessly seek that recklessness that will challenge and seek to change human history until it conforms with the norms of the kingdom of God. And remember the signs of the Christian church have always been the lion, the lamb, the dove, and the fish. But never the chameleon.

The Apostle Paul reminds the believer, "Love must be sincere. Hate what is evil; cling to what is good" (Romans 12:9). He also advised, "Test everything. Hold on to the good. Avoid every kind of evil" (1 Thessalonians 5:21-22).

But, Lord . . .

Father, please teach me to care so much about Your truth that a biblical aversion to sin marks my life. In Jesus' name, Amen.

To Ponder . . .

"Let those who love the LORD hate evil." (Psalm 97:10)

An Illusory Freedom

If the Bible is the trustworthy, authoritative Word of God, then disagreement with what the Bible really teaches is the farthest thing from freedom—it is slavery to self, or circumstances, or sin.

. . . freedom to disagree with the Bible is an illusory freedom; in reality it is bondage to falsehood.

(John R.W. Stott)

Gamalier Bradford, a renowned American biographer who explored the lives and motives of famous individuals, candidly admitted: "I do not read the New Testament for fear of its awakening a storm of anxiety and self-reproach and doubt and dread of having taken the wrong path, of having been traitor to the plain and simple God."

Now the Lord is the Spirit, and where the Spirit of the Lord is, there is freedom.

(2 Corinthians 3:17)

The Knowledge Nugget

As we have seen in these devotionals on the Word of God, the Bible and the Bible alone is God's inerrant communication of His will and heart to fallen men and women. The authority of the Bible is to be foundational. To trust one's *personal experience*, one's *reason* or even one's *church tradition* above the Word of God is a wrong path to take. As the most practical book on this planet, the Bible is composed of exactly sixty-six books in the Old and New Testaments which should be carefully and joyfully studied.

The third person of the Trinity, the Holy Spirit, has been given as our teacher to lead us or illumine our minds in understanding the Word of God, the Bible. As Paul says to the Corinthian believers, "Now the Lord is the Spirit, and where the Spirit of the Lord is, there is freedom" (2 Corinthians 3:17). If the Spirit's primary tool for growing the believer is the Word of God, then true freedom comes from cooperating with Him in the process of understanding and applying that precious communication from God.

Real Life Says . . .

But, of course, not all agree! For example, one liberal scholar expresses the following opinion:

> There is no greater misuse of the Bible than to make it our taskmaster, a body of writing to which we are enslaved. I can see no validity whatsoever to the claim that something written two or three thousand years ago has any special relevance to my way of living and thinking. I happen to buy most of what Jesus said but not because it's in the Bible or because he said it, but rather because I find it existentially valid. And I have to be candid enough to say that there are a few things Jesus said that I can't buy.

The scholar has chosen his words carefully. He thinks it is a misuse of the Bible to make it our "taskmaster." We are not to be "enslaved" by it, he says. He misses the biblical definition of freedom, for freedom, as someone has said, is not the right to do what I want but the power to do what I should. The psalmist understood this concept when he wrote: "I run in the path of your commands, for you have set my heart *free*" (Psalm 119:32, emphasis added). Dietrich Bonhoeffer, a German pastor who was executed during the Nazi regime, once stated, "The demand for absolute liberty brings men to the depths of slavery."

The liberal scholar goes on to say that it is unreasonable to think that something written two or three thousand years ago would be relevant to our lives today. He is absolutely *right* if all that we have in the Bible are the random musings of fallible men and women talking about their ideas about God. But he is dead wrong if the Bible is God's communication to us of His mind and will. And to proclaim that "there are a few things Jesus said that I can't buy" sounds bold and courageous *if* Jesus were only a human being who taught people to be nice to one another. But if He was and is the Son of God, God manifest in flesh, then disagreement with Jesus is disagreement with God. And that's not freedom—that's *foolishness*!

But, Lord . . .

Father, thank You for the freedom, the liberty, which comes through Your Word as the Spirit applies it to my life. I praise You for rescuing me from the wrong path. In Jesus' name, Amen.

To Ponder . . .

Man's first duty is not to find freedom, but a Master!

An Invitation to Study the Gospels

The doctrine of the Bible teaches that God has communicated to us what we need to know about Him and His will for mankind. The second person of the Trinity, the Lord Jesus Christ, came to earth and lived a perfect life which we should study and, by His power, follow.

Jesus Christ alone stands at the absolute center of humanity, the one completely harmonious man. He is the absolute and perfect truth, the highest that humanity can reach; at once its perfect image and supreme Lord.

(Charles W. French)

Jesus alone is able to offer Himself as the sufficient illustration of His own doctrine.

(Herbert Hensley Henson)

Whoever claims to live in him must walk as Jesus did.

(1 John 2:6)

The Knowledge Nugget

Composed of the sixty-six books of the Old and New Testaments, the Word of God is trustworthy, practical and relevant to the needs of men and women today. Many get their beliefs from personal experience, reason, church tradition or revelation. Only the supernatural revelation of God, the Bible, deserves to be one's final authority for what one believes.

When studied carefully and systematically, the Bible grants true wealth, wisdom, strength for suffering and joy. Although it is not a systematic theology book, the doctrines of the Christian faith are explained and illustrated throughout the Bible's stories (narratives), poetry, wisdom literature and teaching sections. Grasping an overall doctrine, such as the doctrine of God, involves studying all the relevant Scriptures and putting that information into understandable categories. All other sources of information outside the Bible are to be judged *by* the Bible when the two are discussing the same topic. For example, if modern psychology says that man's nature is basically good, the Bible's consistent witness of man's sinful nature is to be preferred to human wisdom. There are, however, areas where the Bible does not specifically give us information (for example, what drugs will prevent a heart attack), and the Christian does not need to fear learning the facts of nature or science, for they are gifts of God to His creation.

During the summers I teach a six-week intensive New Testament Greek course in seminary. The students who enroll in that class spend five hours a day, Monday through Friday, for six weeks studying the language of the New Testament. They have *five to six hours* of homework every night! (Aren't you glad you don't have to take my course?)

In the process of that challenging period of study, the students *begin* to learn to translate the New Testament for themselves. After they have gotten a lot of the difficult grammar under their belts, we begin to work our way through some of the easier Greek in the New Testament, the first epistle of John. One of the more difficult verses they take on is First John 2:6, which is translated: "The one who continually says that he continually abides in Him ought (even himself) to continually walk even as that one walked" (my translation). That's a little awkward, but the students see that John's point is a very practical one. If I claim to be a follower of Christ, then I need to know how

He lived so that my life can start to look like His. And the way I learn how *He* lived is by studying the four Gospels!

Real Life Says . . .

Because the world around us does not see the Bible as the Word of God, people have no real reason to take it seriously or to study it intensely. But the Christian does! God has been manifest in the flesh and walked on planet earth for thirty years, providing the model of godly living which every Christian should study carefully! That invitation to study the Gospels is issued to everyone who claims "he lives in Him."

But, Lord . . .

Father, I praise You that You have given me a permanent and accessible record of how life ought to be lived to Your glory. And the central figure in that record is none other than Your Son, the Lord Jesus Christ. Thank You for the four Gospels, for the reliability of their testimony to the sinless life of my Savior. Encourage me to get serious about "walking in His steps." In Jesus' name, Amen.

To Ponder . . .

You've got an invitation to study the earthly life of His Son. How will you RSVP?

Section Three:

Great Is the
God We Adore

A Brief Preview

"Pity the poor atheist who sees a beautiful sunset. Alas, he has no one to thank!"

In this third section we'll discover the Bible's "grand assumption" about the existence of God, ponder the issues of atheism and agnosticism and discover that the God of the Bible is decidedly not "safe" (but He is good). We'll learn that even though God is all-powerful, He cannot do *all* things. We'll discover that God sometimes hides Himself (even from His own people!), and that He is sovereign over evil. We will also look at His characteristics (or attributes) of mercy, holiness and eternity.

We'll discuss how we are to worship the God of the Bible and seek to please Him, for He can indeed be pleased by His people. We'll learn that the Christian is in the introduction business, for the believer is not to allow the true God to remain anonymous in the minds of this world's seekers. And we'll talk about how we who follow Jesus Christ will one day see the true God face-to-face.

The Bible's Grand Assumption

The Bible assumes the existence of the Creator, for His existence explains everything apart from sin.

For my own part, the sense of spiritual relief that comes from rejecting the idea of God as a supernatural being is enormous.

(Julian Huxley)

For an atheist to find God is as difficult as for a thief to find a policeman . . . and for the same reason.

(Anonymous)

In the beginning God created the heavens and the earth. . . . Then God said, "Let us make man in our image, in our likeness."

(Genesis 1:1, 26)

The Knowledge Nugget

The story is told of a college student in a philosophy class, where a class discussion was going on about whether or not God exists. The professor used the following logic: "Has anyone in this class heard God?" Nobody spoke. "Has anyone in this class touched God?" Again, nobody spoke. "Has anyone in this class seen God?" When nobody spoke for the third time, he simply stated, "Then there is no God."

The student did not like the sound of this at all, and asked for permission to speak. The professor granted it, and the student stood up and asked the following questions of his classmates: "Has anyone in this class *heard* our professor's brain?" Silence. "Has anyone in this class *touched* our professor's brain?" Absolute silence. "Has anyone in this class *seen* our professor's brain?" When nobody in the class dared to speak, the student concluded, "Then, according to our professor's logic, it must be true that our professor has no brain!"

He got an "A" for the course.

The issue of proofs for the existence of God is an ongoing debate. The grand assumption of the Bible is that He not only exists, but also evidences His continuing care for His creation every day. The very next beat of our hearts, the very next lungful of air that we breathe, are gifts of God. When the unbeliever Julian Huxley said, "For my own part, the sense of spiritual relief that comes from rejecting the idea of God as a supernatural being is enormous," we should not be surprised. Many in our world do not want the God of the Bible to be the real God.

To provide reasons for believing in the existence of God is important and will be pursued in the next few devotionals. The fact is, however, that those in Bible times would have generally felt such a discussion foolish and irreverent. The people of Israel in the Old Testament saw the mighty acts of God; the people of the New Testament conversed with God-become-man (the Lord Jesus). It is testimony to our worship of science that this society demands reasons to believe in God.

Real Life Says . . .

For many in our world today, the very idea of believing in the God of the Bible seems to be on the level of therapeutic folklore. "If believing in Him gets you through the day," they might say, "enjoy yourself!" Many consider themselves too bright to "need" such mundane beliefs; others have experienced tragedies that cause them to question the existence of a good, loving God (an issue we will touch on in Day 20 in this section).

For the believer in Jesus Christ, the evidences of God's existence are everywhere: in nature, in circumstances and in the Christian's own life. How absurd to demand proof of a loved one's existence! C.S. Lewis reminds us that God has "more to do than simply exist"!

Stephen Brown tells the story of the Russian cosmonaut who said when he came back from space: "I looked for God and I didn't see Him!" One writer commented, "If he had left his space capsule and removed his spacesuit, *then* he would have seen God!" The path to discovering the existence of the God of the Bible does not have to be the path of *death*, thankfully, for at that point it is too late!

But, Lord . . .

Father, forgive me when I forget Your mighty acts in history and in my own life. Help me to live in such a way that others will be drawn to You by the evidence of my life. In Jesus' name, Amen.

To Ponder . . .

The world embarrasses me, and I cannot think that this watch exists and has no watchmaker. (Voltaire)

"We've Still Got a Universe on Our Hands, Haven't We?"

God does not depend on mankind for His existence as Creator and Sustainer of the universe.

The Cosmos is all that is or ever was or ever will be. If we must worship a power greater than ourselves, does it not make sense to revere the Sun and the stars?

(Carl Sagan)

If God did not exist, it would be necessary to invent Him.

(Voltaire)

The God who made the world and everything in it is the Lord of heaven and earth and does not live in temples built by hands. And he is not served by human hands, as if he needed anything, because he himself gives all men life and breath and everything else.

(Acts 17:24-25)

The Knowledge Nugget

How should the Christian respond to a world addicted to idolatry? In Acts 17, the Apostle Paul came to the great city of Athens and was immediately confronted with idols everywhere. He was "greatly distressed" (17:16) at the presence of all those monuments to men's myths, and began to preach the good news about Jesus Christ.

One might expect a message of condemnation and judgment, but Paul showed great wisdom when he said, "You folks are really religious! With your numerous idols, you've even erected an altar with the inscription, 'to an unknown god.' " He did not preach hellfire and brimstone to those lost people, but used their religiosity as a springboard for proclaiming Christ. "What you worship as unknown," he said, "I am going to proclaim to you" (17:23). Paul used their intense religiosity to speak about the true God.

He began his testimony by describing the biblical God as the one and only Creator: "The God who made the world and everything in it is the Lord of heaven and earth and does not live in temples built by hands" (17:24). In referring to God's *transcendence*, Paul emphasized the true God's independent existence. He does not need our belief to exist! And He cannot be contained by the religious buildings which we build.

Paul next spoke of God's need of man: "And he is not served by human hands, as if he needed anything, because he himself gives all men life and breath and everything else" (17:25). When we speak of the *self-sufficiency* of God, we are emphasizing the fact that He does not need man or man's efforts or man's worship in order for Him to be God.

Real Life Says . . .

The late scientist Carl Sagan once said, "The Cosmos is all that is or ever was or ever will be. If we must worship a power greater than ourselves, does it not make sense to revere the Sun and the stars?" But why settle for only a power greater than ourselves? Isn't it more reasonable to pursue the Creator of the sun and the stars?

For many today there is the belief that God needs man, that God's very existence is on the level of Peter Pan: there must be belief in Him in order for Him to exist. As Paul made abundantly clear, the true God is the one and only Creator, and His is an independent existence. His reality is the grand fact of the universe. Man's belief or unbelief in Him does not alter His being—or His care for His creation.

The story is told by Harry Emerson Fosdick of a student who came to see him when Fosdick was the pastor at Riverside Church. "I don't believe in God," said the student. "So you're an atheist," said Fosdick. "Describe for me the God you don't believe in." The student was surprised but he did a good job, picturing God as only a kind of venerable bookkeeper who takes note of everyone's good and bad deeds. When the young man finished, Fosdick said, "My boy, that makes two of us. I don't believe in that God either. But we've still got the universe on our hands, haven't we?"

But, Lord . . .

Father, I thank You for Your masterful job of creating and sustaining this universe. Forgive me when I act as if Your existence is dependent on anything I do or think or believe. Help me today to rejoice in Your power—and Your grace. In Jesus' name, Amen.

To Ponder . . .

To say that God is self-sufficient does not mean that God is self-centered. His love reaches to all who desire it.

The Arrogance of Atheism

The atheist knows too little to categorically declare that the God of the Bible does not exist.

The best reply to an atheist is to give him a good dinner and ask him if he believes there is a cook.

(Louis Nizer)

If a man without a sense of smell declared that this yellow rose I hold had no scent, we should know that he was wrong. The defect is in him, not in the flower. It is the same with a man who says there is no God. It merely means that he is without the capacity to discern His presence.

(Sir Ralph Richardson)

The fool says in his heart,
    "There is no God."
They are corrupt, their deeds are vile;
    there is no one who does good.

(Psalm 14:1)

The Knowledge Nugget

There is a fairly straightforward way to move someone from the category of "atheist" (one who declares there is no God) to the category of "agnostic" (one who says he does not know whether there is a God). Ask three simple questions: The first question is, "Of all the knowledge that we could ever achieve as a human race, what percentage do you think we've attained at this point in history?" Perhaps he says, "Only ten percent. We now know only ten percent of all there is to ever know." The second question is, "Of the knowledge that mankind presently has, how much of that ten percent do you *personally* possess?" Let's imagine that he says, "Oh, I guess I know only one percent of that ten percent." (He would be a genius!) The third question is, "Would you not agree that *outside your present knowledge* (one percent of that ten percent) it is at least *possible* that evidence for the God of the Bible exists?" An honest atheist has to say, "Yes, I guess it is *possible*."

You might then carefully comment, "Congratulations. You've now moved from the category of *atheist* to the category of *agnostic*, someone who says he does not know if God exists. My real question for you now is, 'What kind of agnostic are you?' " He might reply, "What do you mean, 'What kind of agnostic am I?' " You might say, "Well, there are two kinds of agnostics. There are those who say, 'I don't know if God exists, but I'd like to see any evidence which you have.' We might term this the *eager agnostic*. There is also the kind who says, 'I don't know if God exists, and *I really don't care!*' We might call this second person an *apathetic agnostic*. Which are you?"

Admittedly, there is one problem with this line of reasoning (which we will deal with in our next devotional). The point of the matter, however, still stands: the atheist knows far too little to be so dogmatic! The Bible declares that only a fool says in his heart, "there is no God" (Psalm 14:1).

Real Life Says . . .

For many in our world the question of God's existence will never be finally answered this side of eternity. Despite the arguments from design, cause and effect, the nature of man and the incarnation of

God Himself, many people would prefer to believe that the existence of the God of the Bible is unknown and unknowable.

C.S. Lewis ridicules atheism by writing, "Atheism turns out to be too simple. If the whole universe has no meaning, we should have never found out that it has no meaning: Just as, if there were no light in the universe and therefore no creatures with eyes, we should never know it was dark. 'Dark' would be without meaning."

Sir Ralph Richardson reminds us that the defect to detect the reality of God is in the atheist himself. And that is where the believer in Jesus Christ comes in. Our task is to demonstrate God's reality to a needy world.

But, Lord . . .

Father, we are an arrogant creation! We demand that You prove Your existence to Your own creatures! Thank You that You have done exactly that in the person of Your Son, the Lord Jesus Christ. Help me today to demonstrate to a lost world the reality of not only Your existence, but also of Your love. In Jesus' name, Amen.

To Ponder . . .

The great scholar Augustine once commented, "No man says, 'There is no God' but he whose interest it is that there should be none."

The Sadness of Agnosticism

The agnostic says that he does not know if the God of the Bible exists. Despite the problem of evil in the world, the evidence of God's reality is abundant.

In a book entitled *Children's Answers to Sunday School Questions*, one child wrote: "It is sometimes difficult to hear what is being said in church because the *agnostics* are so terrible."

Father, the pagans ask, "If there is a good God, why is there so much evil in the world?" But once we're a part of Your family, the question changes. "If there is a just God, why is there so much good in the world?"

(Stephen Brown)

I consider everything a loss compared to the surpassing greatness of knowing Christ Jesus my Lord. . . . I want to know Christ and the power of his resurrection and the fellowship of sharing in his sufferings.

(Philippians 3:8, 10)

The Knowledge Nugget

I heard of one fellow who said, "I'm a paranoid agnostic. I doubt the existence of God, but whatever is there, it's out to get me!" In yesterday's devotional, we looked at several questions which one could ask an atheist in order to move him from denying the existence of God to the position of agnosticism (that is, someone who does not know if God exists, but would like to know). The *eager agnostic* wants to look at the Christian's evidence for God; the *apathetic agnostic* chooses not to do any investigating.

There is one objection to the questions posed in yesterday's devotional. What if the ten percent knowledge of the atheist seems to show him that, if there is a God, He must be evil because He allows so much suffering and disaster in His world? Unlike many other world religions, biblical Christianity does not deny the existence of evil and suffering, but rather proclaims a God who entered into His own suffering world (in the person of Jesus Christ) and took upon Himself the sin of all humanity. As the great Christian author Dorothy Sayers puts it, "God did not abolish the fact of evil: He transformed it. He did not stop the crucifixion: He rose from the dead."

The atheist might use the same logic on you to try to convince you that outside of your knowledge, there might be evidence that God *does not exist*! How should you respond? With the evidence for God's existence, of course. Honestly admit the slim possibility that God may not exist, but the best evidence available (especially regarding Christ) demonstrates His reality.

We will notice some of the evidences for God-become-man in the devotionals on the Person of Christ in the next book. The Apostle Paul speaks to the issue of agnosticism in Philippians 3 and joyfully declares, "I consider everything a loss compared to the surpassing greatness of knowing Christ Jesus my Lord. . . . I want to know Christ and the power of his resurrection and the fellowship of sharing in his sufferings" (Philippians 3:8, 10).

Real Life Says . . .

If there is a God, says the world, He is so distant from us that He is unknowable. Or the existence of evil and suffering in life calls His existence into question (an issue we address in Day 20). The Bible teaches that God has made Himself finally known through His Son, the Lord Jesus Christ.

The Christian Akbar Abdul-Haqq once wrote: "So you think that God does not exist anywhere? You must have a great deal of knowledge about the universe. Apparently you have examined every nook and corner of it. Logically it is impossible to say, 'There is no God.' All you can say is, 'There is no God in my experience.' I have found God in Christ. That is my experience. You can have it too. But not your way. You must try God's way."

But, Lord . . .

Father, how sad life must be for those who have not yet found You. Thank You for the abundant evidences not only of Your reality, but also of Your love and care for Your creation. Use me to cause the agnostics I know to long to know You. In Jesus' name, Amen.

To Ponder . . .

The story is told of a brilliant but bitter agnostic writer who toured Europe with his wife and small son. He received honors from schools, royalty and friends. After the family returned home, his son, impressed with his father's fame, said, "Daddy, I guess pretty soon you will know everybody, except God."

Not Safe, but Good

God's attribute of goodness, His moral purity, should cause us to trust Him in all circumstances of life.

Erma Bombeck once responded to an RSVP to a pro-am ski tournament: "I do not participate in any sport with ambulances at the bottom of the hill."

The more I considered Christianity, the more I found that while it had established a rule and order, the chief aim of that order was to give room for good things to run wild.

(G.K. Chesterton)

Oh, that men would give thanks to the LORD for His goodness, and for His wonderful works to the children of men!

(Psalm 107:8, NKJV)

The Knowledge Nugget

In the enjoyable series of children's stories, *The Chronicles of Narnia*, C.S. Lewis tells us about Aslan the lion (who represents Christ). When Lucy, one of the main characters, hears that she is going to meet Aslan, she says, "Ooh! . . . I'd thought he was a man. Is he—quite safe? I shall feel rather nervous about meeting a lion."

"That you will, dearie, and no mistake," said Mrs. Beaver [the animals talk in these stories], "if there's anyone who can appear before Aslan without their knees knocking, they're either braver than most or else just silly."

"Then he isn't safe?" said Lucy.

"Safe?" said Mr. Beaver. "Don't you hear what Mrs. Beaver tells you? Who said anything about safe? 'Course he isn't safe. But he's good. He's the King, I tell you."

The theme of God's goodness sweetens all of Scripture. We read in Psalm 34 the challenge to "taste and see that the LORD is good; blessed is the man who takes refuge in him" (34:8). "Good and upright is the LORD," says the psalmist; "therefore he instructs sinners in his ways" (25:8). "You are forgiving and good, O Lord, abounding in love to all who call to you" (86:5). "You are good, and what you do is good; teach me your decrees" (119:68).

In the New Testament, the same theme continues: "I am the good shepherd. The good shepherd lays down his life for the sheep" (John 10:11). It is the "goodness" (KJV) of God that brings men, or should bring men, to repentance (Romans 2:4 ["kindness" in NIV]).

Real Life Says . . .

The world around us has no real way of dealing with the thorny issue of suffering and evil in this world *if* people reject the biblical witness of God's goodness. Although we will speak more of the need to defend God's goodness in the face of evil's reality, at this point we must recognize the Bible's consistent testimony to the goodness of God.

I was saved when I was a teenager, but I struggled with really surrendering to the Lord and His will for my life. I feared that if I ever said, "Lord, I am totally Yours. I'll go anywhere You want me to go, do anything You want me to do," I would immediately hear a voice boom from heaven: "*Aha!* NOW I've got you! And I'm going to make your life *miserable!* I'm going to send you to some dark part of the world where you'll have to eat what human beings were never intended to eat!" I'm convinced my struggle was partially due to a misunderstanding of the doctrine of God's *goodness*.

Our standards of good and bad are sometimes determined arbitrarily, arrived at via democratic vote, or just aren't clear at all. Good and bad are crystal clear to God. And He does not conform Himself and His standards to something outside Himself; *He* is the standard for good and bad, right and wrong. Goodness flows from His very character, His very being. With the psalmist we should declare, "Oh, that men would give thanks to the Lord for His goodness, and for His wonderful works to the children of men!" (Psalm 107:8, NKJV).

But, Lord . . .

Father, I've been a victim of the Evil One's propaganda campaign. Please forgive me for doubting Your goodness—and help me today to rejoice in You and to obey You even when the evidences of Your goodness are not apparent to me. In Jesus' name, Amen.

To Ponder . . .

Because *God* is good, John Wesley's challenge to the Christian makes perfect sense: "Do all the good you can by all the means you can in all the ways you can in all the places you can in all the times you can to all the people you can as long as ever you can."

The Theology of an Afterthought

God's knowledge of us provides the foundation for our spiritual growth and our concern for evangelism.

God and I have this in common—we both love His Son, Jesus Christ.

(Lance Zavitz)

Every man naturally desireth to know; but what doth knowledge avail without the fear of God?

(Thomas à Kempis)

Formerly, when you did not know God, you were slaves to those who by nature are not gods. But now that you know God—or rather are known by God—how is it that you are turning back to those weak and miserable principles? Do you wish to be enslaved by them all over again?

(Galatians 4:8-9)

The Knowledge Nugget

A world-renowned Christian university has as its motto: "To know Him . . . and to make Him known." A personal walk with Jesus Christ ("to know Him") underlies the curriculum, and a heart for getting the gospel out to the lost ("to make Him known") characterizes almost everything the university does. Many who are trained there give themselves to serving the Savior on mission fields throughout the world.

As commendable as such a motto is, there is another dimension which is as important (if not more important) than growing in one's personal knowledge of Christ or sharing the gospel with the nations. What could possibly be more important than those two callings?

The Apostle Paul writes to the Galatian believers who were once enslaved by idolatry, but had been freed by the good news about Jesus' saving work. He declared, "Now that you know God—or rather *are known by God* . . ." (Galatians 4:9, emphasis added; see also 1 Corinthians 8:3). I call this "the theology of an afterthought." What is more important than my knowing God? *His knowing me!* What is more important than my making Christ known to the world? *His knowing me!*

This is not to say that we can glide to glory, neither growing in our relationship with Christ nor introducing others to Him. In fact, being known by God is the *foundation* of the other two.

The psalmist expresses this best when he writes about God's omniscience:

> O LORD, you have searched me
> and you know me.
> You know when I sit and when I rise;
> you perceive my thoughts from afar.
> You discern my going out and my lying down;
> you are familiar with all my ways.
> Before a word is on my tongue
> you know it completely, O LORD.
>
> You hem me in—behind and before;
> you have laid your hand upon me.
> Such knowledge is too wonderful for me,
> too lofty for me to attain. (Psalm 139:1-6)

God knows our bodily positions, what we are thinking, where we are going and when we are lying down. He does not have to guess what we're going to say—He knows it before we can manipulate tongue and vocal cords to convert those thoughts into words. He has hemmed us in—surrounded us. His hand has been "laid upon" us—not in discipline, but in intimacy. As Cynthia Heald puts it, "God does not have a secret society of intimate friends. We are as intimate with God as *we* choose to be."

Real Life Says . . .

A cynical world not only doubts the existence of the biblical God, but it also believes that, if He does exist, He cannot be known or loved. But the world is wrong, for "the LORD knows the thoughts of man; he knows that they are futile" (Psalm 94:11).

I understand that medical professionals have been ribbing each other for years about their respective callings. The surgeon, it is said, does everything but doesn't know anything. The internist knows everything but doesn't do anything. The psychiatrist doesn't know or do anything. And the pathologist knows everything but it's too late! When it comes to the real God, He not only knows everything, but He also can do anything which does not violate His own nature. And that is comforting news for His child and terrifying news for those who resist His grace.

But, Lord . . .

Father, Great Knower of my heart, forgive me when I act as though I must bring You up-to-date with the events of my life. You know them before I form them into words. Help me to bask in Your knowledge and grace today. In Jesus' name, Amen.

To Ponder . . .

He sees all things; even the steps of a black ant on a black rock in a dark night. (Islam's description of Allah)

God Cannot Do ALL Things

The doctrine of God's all-powerfulness (omnipotence) means that He can do all things that are consistent with His nature. He cannot violate His own character or being.

The greatest single distinguishing feature of the omnipotence of God is that our imagination gets lost when thinking about it.

(Pascal)

Jesus is all we have; He is all we need and all we want. We are shipwrecked on God and stranded on omnipotence!

(Vance Havner)

I am the LORD, the God of all mankind. Is anything too hard for me?

(Jeremiah 32:27)

The Knowledge Nugget

The story is told of a young boy who was taking a train to visit his grandfather. In the seat next to him was a seminary professor. The young boy was reading a Sunday school take-home paper, and the prof thought he would have some fun with the boy. So he said,

"Young man, if you can tell me something that God can do, I'll give you a big shiny apple."

Thoughtfully the boy replied, "Mister, if you can tell me something God *can't* do, I'll give you a whole *barrel* of apples." The believer in Jesus Christ can have complete confidence in the complete competence of God!

Occasionally, an unbeliever will pose the question, "Can God create a rock heavier than He can lift?" Be careful with this question! If you say, "Certainly! God can do anything. Of course He can create such a rock," the unbeliever will say, "Aha! But it is a rock that He *cannot* lift! *So He is not omnipotent!*" You quickly do an about-face, "Well, no, He cannot create such a rock!" The unbeliever responds, "Aha! So He *cannot* create a rock heavier than He can lift! *Then He is not all-powerful*, for there is something He cannot do!"

The best response to such a question is to say, "That's a bad question." For either way you answer it, you lose. It is a question similar to "Have you stopped beating your dog?" No matter which way you answer, you're guilty either of having beaten or continuing to beat your dog!

But is there anything that God cannot do? We read in Luke 1 of God's allowing Elizabeth (John the Baptist's mother) to become pregnant, even though she was barren. The angel Gabriel gives this information to Mary to remind her that "nothing is impossible with God" (Luke 1:37). The God who can cause the barren woman to become pregnant can also cause a young virgin to conceive without the participation of a human male.

Real Life Says . . .

"If God can do all things," some might say, "then can He *sin*? Can He *cease to exist*?" We must point out here that the Bible is crystal clear that God's omnipotence does not violate His holy character or nature.

For example, we read in Hebrews 6:18 that it "is impossible for God to lie."

God cannot be anything other than faithful. Paul reminded Timothy that "if we are faithless, he will remain faithful, for *he cannot disown himself*" (2 Timothy 2:13, emphasis added). We read in James that "every good and perfect gift is from above, coming down from the Father of the heavenly lights, who *does not change like shifting shadows*" (James 1:17, emphasis added). John tells us that "God is light; *in him there is no darkness at all*" (1 John 1:5, emphasis added). John used the strongest language available in Greek to say there is no darkness in God, no, *none at all*. As we saw in the devotional on the goodness of God (Day 5 in this section), the Bible consistently maintains God's absolute purity and holiness.

God's inability to do anything contrary to His own nature is not a vice, but a virtue. Aren't you glad that God cannot lie, cannot deny Himself, cannot cease to be who He is? The prophet Malachi reminds us that God is the always faithful One, the One who keeps His promises to His people. Malachi writes, "I the LORD do not change. So you, O descendants of Jacob, are not destroyed" (3:6).

But, Lord . . .

Father, I praise You for Your all-powerfulness which expresses Your perfect character and holy nature. Thank You that You cannot deny Yourself. By Your Holy Spirit mold my life so that it reveals, however imperfectly, something of Your grace. In Jesus' name, Amen.

To Ponder . . .

God's inability to be anything other than perfection gives us confidence in the storms of life.

More Than Trembling Monotheists

The Bible teaches that God is one (this is called *monotheism***), and that fact should move us from fear to focused living for His glory.**

It is the experience of the unbeliever to tremble at the rustling of a leaf.

(Martin Luther)

If Christianity has never frightened us, we have not yet learned what it is.

(William Temple)

You believe that there is one God. Good! Even the demons believe that—and shudder.

(James 2:19)

The Knowledge Nugget

We read in the Old Testament book of Deuteronomy the cry: "Hear, O Israel: The LORD our God, the LORD is one. Love the LORD your God with all your heart and with all your soul and with all your strength" (Deuteronomy 6:4-5). This great theological declaration is called the *Shema*, from the Hebrew word meaning "Hear!"

The oneness of God is a fundamental teaching of the Bible and, according to Moses, is to be taught to our children "when you sit at home and when you walk along the road, when you lie down and when you get up" (6:7).

On one occasion, Jesus had to meet the theological challenges of two specific groups. He successfully answered the Sadducees (who denied the doctrine of the resurrection) by emphasizing the fact that God is "the God of Abraham, the God of Isaac, and the God of Jacob. He is not the God of the dead, but of the living" (Mark 12:26-27). He is then quizzed by the Pharisees (a group dedicated to keeping God's law), using the question, "What is the most important commandment?"

> "The most important one," answered Jesus, "is this: 'Hear, O Israel, the Lord our God, the Lord is one. Love the Lord your God with all your heart and with all your soul and with all your mind and with all your strength.' The second is this: 'Love your neighbor as yourself.' There is no commandment greater than these." (12:29-31)

Several key ideas stand out in Jesus' answer. First, He repeats the *Shema*, emphasizing the fundamental truth of God's oneness. Second, He spells out the practical application of that command which is to love God with all of one's being. Third, He brings in the commandment to love one's neighbor as oneself (a commandment which is mentioned neither in Deuteronomy 6 nor in Exodus 20 when the ten commandments were first given).

Jesus' point seems to be that the Sadducees had missed the living God altogether. But the Pharisees, who acknowledged God's oneness, were denying the implication of that truth by loving neither God nor neighbor. Their belief in God's oneness was empty and void.

Real Life Says . . .

We live in a design-your-own-god culture, so the question of monotheism is a largely irrelevant one to many today. But if God's oneness is a fundamental description of the true God, then all other gods are mere idols. And simply acknowledging the oneness of God is not enough. If He is not loved and obeyed, then such belief, even if shouted from the housetops, is mere words. A love for the true God must lead to a love for one's neighbor.

The New Testament writer James hits hard on the issue of belief divorced from love and good deeds. In his second chapter, he rails against those who think that "mere faith"—a faith that leads to no life change, that does not reach out in compassion to hurting fellow-believers—is sufficient. To all who so contrast faith and deeds that they have an inactive, strictly internal conception of God, an orthodoxy that is only verbal, he says, "Big deal! You pride yourself on your affirmation of monotheism. So what? The demons are also monotheists! And they even do you one better. They *tremble* before the one and only God" (James 2:19, author paraphrase). God is not looking for mere monotheists. He is looking for obedient and loving sons and daughters.

But, Lord . . .

Father, I understand that great doctrinal truth can bring great spiritual danger. When I think that mere belief is enough, that You are pleased with right thoughts alone, I am missing the mark. Help me by Your Spirit to practice what I proclaim. In Jesus' name, Amen.

To Ponder . . .

A true monotheism will show itself in a sold-out, whole-life love of God and a sacrificial love of one's neighbor. If not, it is merely the doctrine of demons.

The Truth of the Trinity

The belief in one God eternally existent as three persons is taught in the Bible and should be embraced and acknowledged by all genuine Christians.

Explain the Trinity? We can't even begin. We can only accept it—a mystery, disclosed in Scripture. It should be no surprise that the triune Being of God baffles our finite minds. We should be surprised, rather, if we *could* understand the nature of our Creator. He would be a two-bit deity, not the fathomless Source of all reality.

(Vernon Grounds)

God, to keep us sober, speaks sparingly of His essence.

(John Calvin)

May the grace of the Lord Jesus Christ, and the love of God, and the fellowship of the Holy Spirit be with you all.

(2 Corinthians 13:14)

The Knowledge Nugget

"But the word 'Trinity' isn't even *in* the Bible!" said the nicely dressed young Jehovah's Witness who was standing on my front porch. Perhaps you've had the same thing happen to you. Why do we Christians believe in the doctrine of the Trinity, and does such a controversial belief really matter?

We believe in God's unity or oneness (as we saw in yesterday's devotional) and therefore reject any notion of more than one God in the universe. Christians are *not* polytheists (a belief in more than one God). But doesn't the doctrine of the Trinity sound like a belief in *three* gods?

First of all, it must be said that we affirm the doctrine of the Trinity despite the fact that the term does not occur in the Bible. Other terms important to us do not occur in the Bible either, such as "theocracy" (government by God—a favorite term of Jehovah's Witnesses, by the way), "theodicy" (a defense of God's goodness in the face of evil's reality) or "Sunday school" (we all know what that term means!). The issue is not whether the word itself appears in the Bible, but whether the *concept* is a biblical one. The great scholar Tertullian coined the term "Trinity" to explain the biblical data that asserts God's oneness ("unity") and His plurality ("threeness").

What is the evidence of His "threeness"? Traditional references include Genesis 1:26 ("Let *us* make man in our image," emphasis added), Matthew 3:16-17 (the baptism of Jesus), Matthew 28:19-20 (the Great Commission), as well as benedictions or blessings, such as Second Corinthians 13:14 (which mentions Father, Son and Holy Spirit) and Jude 20-21.

The fact of the matter is that the Bible indicates that the Father is God (Deuteronomy 6:3), the Son is God (John 1:1; 20:28) and the Holy Spirit is God (Acts 5:3-4)—yet there is only one God! The burden is on the one who denies the doctrine of the Trinity to explain such passages, and, believe me, the Jehovah's Witnesses certainly try! For them only Jehovah is the almighty God. Jesus is God's first creation (actually, they believe He is Michael the archangel, who gave up His angelic nature to become man) and the Holy Spirit is neither divine nor a real person (He is Jehovah's "active force"). Such explanations support one kind of strict monotheism, but do little justice to the clear evidences of both Christ's and the Holy Spirit's full deity (subjects we will examine more closely when we discuss the doctrine of Christ and the doctrine of the Holy Spirit).

Real Life Says . . .

Such theological questions seem completely irrelevant to the world around us. But if we are dealing with the very nature of the living and true God, we must take the biblical material seriously. The doctrine of the Trinity explains, for example, how God could love before He created the world. He did not need to create in order to love. There was love between the Father, Son and Holy Spirit before this world came into existence.

But, Lord . . .

Father, I don't understand Your essential being, and I shouldn't expect to. I want to believe what Your Word teaches. Help me to worship You, to proclaim Your Son's finished work on Calvary and to enjoy the fellowship of the Holy Spirit. In Jesus' name, Amen.

To Ponder . . .

Having the wrong view of God means having the wrong view of Jesus. And that is spiritually lethal.

A "Get 'em, Copper!" Kind of Christianity

The mercy of God is defined as the withholding of deserved judgment by God.

Forgiven souls are humble. They cannot forget that they owe all they have and hope for to free grace, and this keeps them lowly. They are brands plucked from the fire—debtors who could not pay for themselves—captives who must have remained in prison for ever, but for undeserved mercy—wandering sheep who were ready to perish when the Shepherd found them . . .

(J.C. Ryle)

God's mercy is a holy mercy, which knows how to pardon sin, not to protect it; it is a sanctuary for the penitent, not for the presumptuous.

(Bishop Reynolds)

Show me your ways, O LORD,
   teach me your paths;
guide me in your truth and teach me,
   for you are God my Savior,
   and my hope is in you all day long.

Remember, O LORD, your great mercy and love,
   for they are from of old.

                                                (Psalm 25:4-6)

The Knowledge Nugget

If grace is God's undeserved favor (as we will see in tomorrow's devotional), mercy is His unmerited compassion. Grace gives us what we do not deserve; mercy withholds from us the judgment we do deserve.

I don't know about you, but one of the more frightening sights for me is, while I'm driving down the highway, to suddenly see flashing lights in my rearview mirror! The last time that happened to me, I immediately slowed down and prayed to the Lord, "O, Father, please don't let me get a ticket! Please let this police officer be an instrument of Your mercy, instead of Your judgment!" As I slowed down, the police car sped past me, obviously hot on the trail of some other wicked offender. My thought as he whizzed by? "Get 'em, Copper!" Interesting how I wanted *mercy* for myself, but *judgment* for the next guy!

The psalmist has much to say about God's mercy. He recognizes the holiness of God and the fact that no human has a right to God's compassion: "If you, O LORD, kept a record of sins, O Lord, who could stand? But with you there is forgiveness; therefore you are feared" (Psalm 130:3-4).

Real Life Says . . .

In our age of victimhood, few people recognize God's right to act in judgment. They believe either that God is too loving to condemn or that man is too good to be condemned—and they are wrong on both counts. Jonathan Edwards' sermon "Sinners in the Hands of an Angry God" makes little sense to them. Many would prefer the title "God in the Hands of Angry Sinners"!

But biblical Christianity teaches that "As a father has compassion [mercy] on his children, so the LORD has compassion on those who fear him" (103:13). He is a God who "is gracious and compassionate, slow to anger and rich in love" (145:8). All of Psalm 136 is an ode to God's mercy, for the phrase "his mercy endureth for ever" (KJV) forms the second half of each of its twenty-six verses. The most famous psalm of them all concludes with the words: "Surely goodness and mercy shall follow me all the days of my life; and I will dwell in the house of the LORD forever" (23:6, KJV).

Although we are often stingy in showing mercy to others, giving sad testimony to the poverty of our compassion, the Apostle Paul speaks quite differently of the Lord: "But because of his great love for us, God, who is rich in mercy, made us alive with Christ even when we were dead in transgressions—it is by grace you have been saved" (Ephesians 2:4-5).

The story is told of a past-her-prime Hollywood star who was sitting for some promotional photos. She barked at the photographer, "I want these pictures to do me justice, young man!" He was heard to say under his breath, "Ma'am, what you need is not justice, but *mercy*." That's what we all need—and his mercies "are new every morning" (Lamentations 3:23) to those in Christ.

But, Lord . . .

Lord, what a mass of contradictions I find in my own life. I take Your mercies for granted and grant little compassion to others. Forgive me by Your abundant mercies. In Jesus' name, Amen.

To Ponder . . .

If God were not willing to forgive sin, heaven would be empty. (German proverb)

"Me... That Worm!"

God's grace is His unmerited favor, His undeserved, unrepaid kindness. Grace is God giving us what He does not owe us—His love.

A woman in a little New England village, upon seeing a magnificent sunset, said, "What a wonderful sunset for such a little place."

The source of strength lies in God's grace, not in our will-power or in our spasms of earnestness. When we attempt to strengthen ourselves through self-effort, we are like the man who tried to make his stalled boat move by pushing against the mast. We exert ourselves a great deal, but actually get nowhere.

(N.A. Woychuk)

For the grace of God that brings salvation has appeared to all men. . . . We wait for the blessed hope—the glorious appearing of our great God and Savior, Jesus Christ, who gave himself for us to redeem us from all wickedness and to purify for himself a people that are his very own, eager to do what is good.

(Titus 2:11, 13-14)

The Knowledge Nugget

An old Indian chief, after living for many years in sin, was led to Christ by a missionary. When asked by his friends to explain the change in his life, he picked up a little worm and placed it on a pile of leaves. He then touched a match to the leaves and watched them smolder and burst into flames. As the flames worked their way up to the center where the worm lay, the old chief suddenly plunged his hand into the center of the burning pile and snatched the worm out. Holding the worm gently in his hand he gave this testimony to the grace of God: "Me . . . that worm!"

Is that how you see yourself? The Bible speaks of Israel being "a burning stick snatched from the fire" (Zechariah 3:2). C.S. Lewis changes the image in order to explain something about the grace of God when he writes,

> I never had the experience of hunting for God. It was the other way around: He was the hunter (or so it seemed to me) and I was the deer. He stalked me like a redskin, took unerring aim, and fired. And I am very thankful that this is how the first (conscious) meeting occurred. It forearms one against subsequent fears that the whole thing was only wish fulfillment. Something one didn't wish for can hardly be that.

God's grace is not wish fulfillment, nor our imagination, nor the way we would expect a righteous God to act. His grace is shown to sinners at the cost of His Son's life. As was quoted yesterday from J.C. Ryle:

> Forgiven souls are humble. They cannot forget that they owe all they have and hope for to free grace, and this keeps them lowly. They are brands plucked from the fire—debtors who could not pay for themselves—captives who must have remained in prison for ever, but for undeserved mercy—wandering sheep who were ready to perish when the Shepherd found them.

Real Life Says . . .

Most in our world do not see themselves in desperate need of God's grace. They do not recognize that they are brands (burning sticks) still in the fire of God's judgment who need to be plucked out. They do not understand the enormous debt they owe to God, a debt they can never repay. And they don't even see the bars of their own prison which keep them from the grace-filled love of God.

But that's where the believer in Christ comes in. We are to be daily object lessons of God's grace. For it is the "grace of God . . . [that] has appeared to all men" (Titus 2:11); it is the grace of God by which any sinner is "justified freely" (Romans 3:24); and it is by God's grace that the believer can stand before a grace-hungry world and proclaim: "Me . . . that worm!"

But, Lord . . .

Father, in our works-oriented world we forget Your unmerited favor. Thank You for Your grace that is abundant, rich and free to all who come to Your Son. In Jesus' name, Amen.

To Ponder . . .

God has no more precious gift to a church or an age than a man who lives as an embodiment of His will and inspires those around him with the faith of what grace can do. (Andrew Murray)

The God Who Hides Himself

The doctrine of God's omnipresence (that He is everywhere) does not rule out the fact that He, at times, hides Himself from His people for His reasons.

Sometimes Thou dost withdraw Thyself from us that we might know the sweetness of Thy presence.

(Thomas à Kempis)

The central idea of the great part of the Old Testament may be called the idea of the loneliness of God.

(G.K. Chesterton)

Truly you are a God who hides himself,
　O God and Savior of Israel.

(Isaiah 45:15)

The Knowledge Nugget

We read in the book of Genesis that Adam and Eve, after they had sinned against God, "hid from the LORD God among the trees of the garden" (Genesis 3:8). The psalmist prays, "Keep me as the apple of your eye; hide me in the shadow of your wings" (Psalm 17:8). He also prays for protection: "Rescue me from my enemies, O LORD, for I hide myself in you" (143:9). Both hiding from God and hiding in God are real conditions of the believer at various times.

But does God ever hide from us? When I was a young Christian, a popular saying was, "If you feel distant from God, guess who moved!" And of course, the *correct* answer was thought to be that God does not move away from us, but we move from Him, either through sin or by losing our zeal for the Lord.

Sometimes God hides Himself from us because of our sin (see Isaiah 64:7). But is it possible that God sometimes hides Himself from His people for other reasons? Isaiah declares that He is "a God who hides himself" (45:15). There is no indication here that He hides Himself because of His people's sin, but perhaps so that His people might seek Him on a deeper and more intimate level.

Real Life Says . . .

Many in our world not only deny God's existence, but they also insist, almost in the same words as those who crucified Jesus, that He "come down now from [heaven], that we may see and believe" (Mark 15:32). God *has* come down from heaven, demonstrating His love for His wayward creation.

For the believer in Christ, those periods when God seems distant, or when He has removed a sense of His presence from us, *may be* because of our sin. On the other hand, this God who sometimes "hides Himself" may simply be seeking to be sought!

A.W. Tozer understood the need to continually seek the Lord, as we earlier noticed:

> Everything is made to center upon the initial act of "accepting" Christ (a term, incidentally, which is not found in the Bible) and we are not expected thereafter to crave any further revelation of God to our souls. We have been snared in the coils of a spurious logic which insists that if we have found Him we need no more seek Him.

When my children were small, I would come home from work, kiss my wife and children hello, and, when their backs were turned, quickly hide in our linen closet. Why would I do such a thing? The kids immediately recognized that Dad was initiating a game of hide-and-seek.

They would look everywhere for me, except that linen closet. After a little while, when the kids were searching some other part of the house, I would slip out and sit at the table, drinking coffee with my wife. The kids would see me, do a double take and say, "Where *were* you?" I would not tell them my secret hiding place.

One day I kissed my family hello, vanished into my linen closet and heard the kids scampering around trying to find me. After a few minutes, the house became silent. When I came out of hiding, I found them downstairs playing with Legos. They had lost interest in finding Dad!

But, Lord . . .

Father, I am sorry for the times that You have hidden Yourself, and I've not noticed that You were missing. Forgive me. In Jesus' name, Amen.

To Ponder . . .

Don't assume that because God knows all things He has no desire to be known Himself.

The Idiocy of Idolatry

Idolatry (the worshiping of any created object, including the thoughts of man) makes no sense in light of the existence of the real God.

I confess I would almost rather be charged with a religion that extenuated murder, than with one that justified idolatry. Murder, great as the offense is, is but the slaying of man; but idolatry is, in its essence, the killing of God.

(Charles Spurgeon)

It's easy to get attached to idols, good things inappropriately adored. But when you have Jesus in the center of a room, everything else only junks up the decor.

(Charles Swindoll)

Of what value is an idol, since a man has carved it?
　Or an image that teaches lies?
For he who makes it trusts in his own creation;
　he makes idols that cannot speak.
Woe to him who says to wood, "Come to life!"
　Or to lifeless stone, "Wake up!"
Can it give guidance?
　It is covered with gold and silver;
　there is no breath in it.
But the LORD is in his holy temple;
　let all the earth be silent before him.

(Habakkuk 2:18-20)

The Knowledge Nugget

The Bible teaches, and much of sociology has discovered, that man is incurably religious. As we learned earlier from G.K. Chesterton, when man ceases to believe in God, he does not believe in nothing. He believes in anything.

Idolatry, said Augustine, is "worshiping anything that ought to be used, or using anything that is meant to be worshiped." And mankind is quite capable of literally worshiping *anything*! The Bible minces no words in ridiculing the idiocy of idolatry. The prophet Isaiah attacks these "alternative" ways of worship, speaking sarcastically of the man who uses one part of his woodpile to warm himself, another part to cook his food and a third part to carve his own god (Isaiah 44:9-17). He mocks the idol-makers' guild by saying, "The craftsman encourages the goldsmith, and he who smooths with the hammer spurs on him who strikes the anvil. He says of the welding, 'It is good.' He nails down the idol so it will not topple" (41:7). You know, there's nothing quite as embarrassing as an idol that falls over—or one that rots (see 40:20).

Isaiah declares that in the day of the Lord "men will throw away to the rodents and bats their idols of silver and idols of gold, which they made to worship" (2:20). In chapter 30 he says that the idols are so useless they will be discarded like a menstrual cloth (30:22).

Jeremiah pulls no punches when he ridicules Israel for saying "to wood, 'You are my father,' and to stone, 'You gave me birth.' They have turned their backs to [the Lord]" (Jeremiah 2:27). The psalmist joins the anti-idol chorus by declaring about idols,

> They have mouths, but cannot speak,
>   eyes, but they cannot see;
> they have ears, but cannot hear,
>   noses, but they cannot smell;
> they have hands, but cannot feel,

feet, but they cannot walk;
nor can they utter a sound with their throats.

(Psalm 115:5-7)

Idols don't even have the power to grunt!

Real Life Says . . .

Because the world has no final authority, everything is "up for grabs" when it comes to what or whom one chooses to worship. Jeremiah declares idolatry to be a sad substitute for knowing the living and true God, saying that idol worship had become a "family affair" in Israel which brought great damage:

> "The children gather wood, the fathers light the fire, and the women knead the dough and make cakes of bread for the Queen of Heaven. They pour out drink offerings to other gods to provoke me to anger. But am I the one they are provoking?" declares the LORD. "Are they not rather harming themselves, to their own shame?" (Jeremiah 7:18-19).

The true God, although He does not literally have ears, eyes or a mouth, is described in the Word of God as hearing His people, seeing their need and speaking forth His truth to all who will listen.

But, Lord . . .

Father, it is hard for me to admit my idolatry. Thank You for Your Word's clear condemnation of those idols of this life which are extremely poor substitutes for Your reality. In Jesus' name, Amen.

To Ponder . . .

Isaiah declares that the one who bows down to an idol "feeds on ashes" (Isaiah 44:20). What a diet!

Holiness: The Beauty of God—Part 1

God's attribute of holiness implies not only His eternal disgust with all that is sinful, but also His active pursuit of turning defiled servants into righteous sons and daughters.

Power is God's hand or arm, omniscience His eye, mercy His bowels, eternity His duration, but holiness is His beauty.

(Stephen Charnock)

Christianity is not the religion of love, but of holy and therefore atoning love, which makes it all the more divine as it makes it less promptly popular.

(P.T. Forsyth)

The LORD Almighty will be exalted by his justice,
    and the holy God will show himself
        holy by his righteousness.

(Isaiah 5:16)

The Knowledge Nugget

When we consider the attribute of holiness, we must admit that we have little idea what true holiness is. A.W. Tozer, one of the twentieth century's most perceptive spiritual writers, draws us back to the biblical doctrine of the holiness of God. He writes,

> God is holy and holiness [is] the moral condition necessary to the health of his universe. . . . Whatever is holy is healthy . . . the holiness of God, the wrath of God and the health of creation are inseparably united. God's wrath is his utter intolerance of whatever degrades and destroys. He hates iniquity as a mother hated the polio that would take the life of the child.

The Bible declares the holiness of God in no uncertain terms. Moses speaks for the Lord to Israel and says, "Be holy because I, the LORD your God, am holy" (Leviticus 19:2). Hannah, in praise to God for removing her barrenness, says, "There is no one holy like the LORD; there is no one besides you; there is no Rock like our God" (1 Samuel 2:2). The psalmist proclaims, "You are enthroned as the Holy One; you are the praise of Israel" (Psalm 22:3); and "The LORD is righteous in all his ways, and holy in all his works" (145:17, KJV). The writer of Proverbs insists that "the fear of the LORD is the beginning of wisdom, and knowledge of the Holy One is understanding" (Proverbs 9:10). The seraphs (a category of angels) proclaim, "Holy, holy, holy is the LORD Almighty; the whole earth is full of his glory" (Isaiah 6:3). In the book of Revelation, John sees four living creatures who day and night without ceasing cry: "Holy, holy, holy is the Lord God Almighty, who was, and is, and is to come" (Revelation 4:8).

Real Life Says . . .

Our world mocks the idea of holiness. The late singer Dean Martin often portrayed a drunk in his comedy sketches. He once said, "I met the Reverend Billy Graham. When I shook his hand, my whole right side became sober!" Like Martin, our culture seems not to have a clue about this fundamental characteristic of the true God. Jonathan Edwards rightly reminds us that "a true love of God must begin with a delight in His holiness, and not with a delight in any other attribute; for no other attribute is truly lovely without this."

For those outside the saving mercy of Jesus Christ, there can be nothing more terrifying than appearing before such a holy God. The commentator Matthew Henry said that "no attribute is more dreadful to sinners than His holiness."

The prophet Isaiah proclaims that "The LORD Almighty will be exalted by his justice, and the holy God will show himself holy by his righteousness" (Isaiah 4:16). What we Christians have in the death of the Lord Jesus Christ is precisely what Isaiah prophesied. The holy God has shown Himself holy by judging mankind's sin in the person of His Son. The Apostle Paul emphasizes that Christ's substitutionary sacrifice is the only means by which God can righteously forgive sinners:

> God presented [Christ] as a sacrifice of atonement, through faith in his blood. He did this to demonstrate his justice, because in his forbearance he had left the sins committed beforehand unpunished—he did it to demonstrate his justice at the present time, so as to be just and the one who justifies those who have faith in Jesus. (Romans 3:25-26)

But, Lord . . .

Father, I thank You for Your holiness. Continue to make me holy by Your Spirit. In Jesus' name, Amen.

To Ponder . . .

Jean-Paul Sartre, the famous existentialist philosopher, is reported to have admitted, "The last thing I want is to be subject to the unremitting gaze of a holy God."

Holiness: The Beauty of God—Part 2

Today's Focus

God's personal righteousness (His holiness) is taught throughout the Bible and provides the basis and motivation for the Christian to obey the command, "Be holy as I am holy."

Holy is the way God is. To be holy He does not conform to a standard. He is that standard.

(A.W. Tozer)

Am I becoming more and more in love with God as a holy God, or with the conception of an amiable being who says, "Oh, well, sin doesn't matter much"?

(Oswald Chambers)

Worship the LORD in the splendor of his holiness. Tremble before him, all the earth!

(1 Chronicles 16:29-30)

The Knowledge Nugget

If God is thoroughly good, and if there is no darkness in Him at all, then His holiness ought to motivate the Christian to righteous living. The doctrine of God's holiness teaches that sin matters a great deal to

God. It matters so much that He gave His only Son to pay the ransom for our sin.

In his excellent book *Your God Is Too Small,* J.B. Phillips challenges a number of nonbiblical understandings of God (such as the Cosmic Policeman, the Grand Old Man, etc.). He writes, "We want, in fact, not so much a Father in heaven as a grandfather in heaven—a senile benevolence who, as they say, 'liked to see young people enjoying themselves' and whose plan for the universe was simply that it might be truly said at the end of the day, 'a good time was had by all.'" But that is not a description of the living and true God. As John Flavel puts it, "So in love is Christ with holiness that He will buy it with His blood for us."

In introducing a men's octet at a concert, the master of ceremonies said, "In this group of eight men, the conductor and I are the only two paid members. The rest are *good for nothing.*" The Christian is not to be good *for nothing,* but because he belongs to a thoroughly holy God there is every reason to seek to reflect His holiness. Holiness—becoming like the Lord—is to be the believer's lifelong quest.

Real Life Says . . .

Holiness is a foreign concept to many today. The psalmist echoes the words of First Chronicles 16:29 when he says that we are to "worship the LORD in the splendor of his holiness" (Psalm 29:2). Aren't you glad it is in the splendor of *His* holiness, and not ours? The same writer repeats his challenge in Psalm 96, adding the words, "tremble before him, all the earth" (96:9). For many in our culture to tremble before anyone is unthinkable. But the holy God of all creation, the Lord of glory, the One who spoke the universe into existence, *He* is the One before whom all the earth will bow. In fact, the Apostle Paul picks up that exact point when he says that at the end of time "every knee [will] bow, in heaven and on earth and under the earth, and every tongue confess that Jesus Christ is Lord, to the glory of God the

Father" (Philippians 2:10-11). This does not indicate universal salvation, but rather forced *submission* to the holy God.

The world needs to see holiness in God's people. One writer quips, "A walloping great congregation is fine, and fun, but what most communities really need is a couple of saints!" (Martin Thornton). God says, "Consecrate yourselves and be holy, because I am the LORD your God. Keep my decrees and follow them. I am the LORD, who makes you holy" (Leviticus 20:7-8). Peter repeats the same challenge when he writes, "But just as he who called you is holy, so be holy in all you do; for it is written, 'Be holy, because I am holy'" (1 Peter 1:15-16). The world awaits demonstrations of God's holiness in God's people.

But, Lord . . .

Father, it is one thing for me to understand and defend the doctrine of Your holiness and quite another for me to become holy. Cause me to realize that such a defense is not primarily verbal. Guide me and grow me by Your Spirit in those areas in which I most need to reflect Your holiness. In Jesus' name, Amen.

To Ponder . . .

All spiritual concepts such as holiness remain more or less elusive until they move visibly before us in some personal form. (J. Sidlow Baxter)

No Darkness Allowed

The moral purity of God is declared throughout Scripture and this doctrine should cause His people to strive for righteousness in their own living, for the image of "light" is used to describe both God and His people.

A little boy attended a church which had beautiful stained-glass windows. He saw that the windows contained pictures of St. Matthew, St. Mark, St. Luke, St. John, St. Paul and others. One day he was asked, "What is a saint?" He replied, "A saint is a person whom the light shines through."

(Donald Barnhouse)

There is a sign on the door of a medical photographer's darkroom in San Diego which reads: "Please keep darkroom door closed. If it is left open, all the dark leaks out."

And this is the message which we have heard from him and are announcing to you, that God is light and there is no darkness in him—no, none at all!

(1 John 1:5, author paraphrase)

The Knowledge Nugget

My family and I used to live in Canada, in the province of Manitoba, an area about as flat as the state of Kansas. The advantage of living in such a flat area is the view: the cloud formations, the sweeping wheat fields, the northern lights, the vast starlit skies, all of which provide clear evidence of God's marvelous creativity. Occasionally, when driving at night, I would completely turn out my headlights and drive in the pitch dark. Why would I do such a thing? Well, the roads were perfectly straight, there were no other cars on the highway, and the view on a clear night of billions of stars was spectacular. And my wife usually had a way of letting me know when to turn the lights back on!

Sometimes we Christians become accustomed to the darkness. And the Bible has much to say about light and darkness. For example, Job 33 says, "He redeemed my soul from going down to the pit, and I will live to enjoy the light. God does all these things to a man—twice, even three times—to turn back his soul from the pit, that the light of life may shine on him" (33:28-30). The psalmist declares, "For you have delivered me from death and my feet from stumbling, that I may walk before God in the light of life" (Psalm 56:13). Those who have trusted in Christ have been "called . . . out of darkness into his wonderful light" (1 Peter 2:9).

Many other biblical texts indicate a dramatic change in status for the Christian. And the Christian's response to God's grace is that he or she would live in the light of God's truth. Ephesians 5 says, "For you were once darkness, but now you are light in the Lord. Live as children of light" (5:8). The rest of that text says that to live in the light means to pursue goodness, righteousness and truth; to find out what pleases the Lord; and to shun and expose darkness (5:9-14).

Real Life Says . . .

The world does not care for the darkness/light analogy used in the Bible, and understandably so! God's Word declares that "men loved darkness instead of light because their deeds were evil" (John 3:19). The Apostle Paul speaks of how God has "rescued us from the dominion of darkness" (Colossians 1:13). But only those who have trusted Jesus

Christ have been rescued by the grace of God. The rest are still in the dark.

The natural man has a tendency to gravitate toward darkness, but the believer in Jesus Christ belongs to a Lord who "wraps himself in light as with a garment" (Psalm 104:2), for He does not have any darkness in Himself at all (1 John 1:5).

But, Lord . . .

Father of lights, You are the one who does not change like shifting shadows. Help me to appreciate Your absolute purity and righteousness. And guard me from the world which seeks to darken the counsel of Your Word. In Jesus' name, Amen.

To Ponder . . .

If you and I are "the light of the world" (Matthew 5:14), then we will shine for His glory and reflect His purity.

Mercy, Mercy Me!

The mercy of God refers to God's withholding judgment on those who deserve it. His holiness demands payment for sin; His mercy led Him to give His Son as the atoning sacrifice for our sins.

Robert Frost, summing up the story of Jonah, said, "After Jonah, you could never trust God not to be merciful again."

(Quoted by Philip Yancey)

You can easily judge the character of a man by how he treats those who can do nothing for him.

(James Miles)

The LORD, the LORD God, merciful and gracious, long-suffering, and abundant in goodness and truth, keeping mercy for thousands, forgiving iniquity and transgression and sin . . .

(Exodus 34:6-7, KJV)

The Knowledge Nugget

If God is as holy (Psalm 29:2; Isaiah 6:3) and mankind as sinful (Jeremiah 17:9; Mark 7:21) as the Bible teaches, then all of humanity desperately needs God's mercy! Many do not realize their need for mercy simply because they don't believe sin is as offensive to God as it is or that God is as righteous as the Bible declares. Worse yet, some actually believe they *deserve* God's mercy!

A mother stood before Napoleon and asked for the pardon of her son. The great emperor said that it was the man's second offense and that justice demanded his death. "I don't ask for justice," said the mother. "I plead for mercy."

"But," said the emperor, "he does not deserve mercy."

"Sir," cried the mother, "it would not be mercy if he deserved it, and mercy is all I ask."

"Well then," said the emperor, "I will have mercy," and her son was saved.

By its very definition, mercy is God withholding from us what we deserve, as we say in Day 10's devotional from this section. Part of the twistedness of our sin is that we believe that we deserve God's favor, or that we can earn His grace. Someone has said that children are innocent and love justice, while most adults are wicked and prefer mercy!

The Bible is full of verses extolling the mercy of God. Note the following passages:

> Have *mercy* on me, O God,
>   according to your unfailing love;
> according to your great compassion
>   blot out my transgressions.
> (Psalm 51:1, emphasis added)

> I will sing of the *mercies* of the LORD for ever ... (89:1, KJV, emphasis added)

> The Lord our God is *merciful* and forgiving, even though we have rebelled against him. (Daniel 9:9, emphasis added)

> Because of the LORD's great love we are not consumed,
>   for his compassions [His *mercies*] never fail.
> They are new every morning; great is your faithfulness.
> (Lamentations 3:22-23)

Real Life Says . . .

Our world does not realize its great need for God's daily mercy, the continual withholding of His judgment. But the believer does. We saw in an earlier devotional that God delights in His own attributes. Jeremiah 9:23-24 confirms this:

> "Let not the wise man boast of his wisdom
>   or the strong man boast of his strength
>   or the rich man boast of his riches,
> but let him who boasts boast about this:
>   that he understands and knows me,
> that I am the LORD, who exercises kindness,
>   justice and righteousness on earth,
>   for in these I delight," declares the LORD.

God *delights* in showing mercy! And He *declares* His character of mercy in other passages. For example, back in Exodus 34 the Lord had Moses hew two more stone tablets to replace the ones he had destroyed when Israel committed idolatry. As the Lord descended before Moses to give him the law again, it was the Lord who proclaimed His name and said, "The LORD, The LORD God, merciful and gracious, longsuffering, and abundant in goodness and truth, keeping mercy for thousands, forgiving iniquity and transgression and sin . . ." (Exodus 34:6-7, KJV).

But, Lord . . .

Father, part of the twistedness of sin is forgetting Your mercy. Thank You that You don't forget to be merciful—to the world, to sinners, to Your children. In Jesus' name, Amen.

To Ponder . . .

I understand that a greeting card company has a new economy line—for people who don't deserve the very best! But when you think about it, none of us do.

Sinners in the Hands of an Angry God—Part 1

Today's Focus

The doctrine of God's wrath reminds us of His holiness and His desire to pardon, rather than punish, sin.

Unless God is angry with sin, let us put a bullet in our collective brain, for the universe is mad.

(Sam Milolaski)

God may not even be, but if He is, one thing is sure, He could not send anyone to hell even if He wanted to. His mercy has His hands of holy wrath tied behind His back.

(John Gerstner, expressing the attitude of many today)

Whoever believes in the Son has eternal life, but whoever rejects the Son will not see life, for God's wrath remains on him.

(John 3:36)

The Knowledge Nugget

When we talk about the wrath of God, various words come to mind such as "anger," "righteous indignation," "holiness" and "judgment."

The theologian J.I. Packer says that God's wrath is "never the capricious, self-indulgent, imitable, morally ignorable thing that human anger so often is. It is, instead, a right and necessary reaction to objective moral evil. God is only angry where anger is called for." Another Christian writer, Arthur Pink, says that God's wrath is "His eternal detestation of all unrighteousness and the displeasure and indignation of Divine equity against evil."

Wrath is a reaction to sin, to evil, to all that stands against the holiness of God. And our present society is fast losing its sense of moral outrage. One judge has said that "a society that loses its sense of outrage is doomed to extinction." H.W. Beecher wrote that "a man that does not know how to be angry does not know how to be good. A man that does not know how to be shaken to his heart's core with indignation over things evil is either a fungus or a wicked man."

Jonathan Edwards, the Great Awakening's scholarly preacher, proclaimed in no uncertain terms the wrath of God in his sermon "Sinners in the Hands of an Angry God." Don't let your high school discussion of that sermon cause you to miss its truth! Concentrating ruthlessly on the image of fire, Edwards writes such statements as:

> There is nothing that keeps wicked men at any one moment out of hell, but the mere pleasure of God.

> The wrath of God burns against [the wicked], their damnation does not slumber; the pit is prepared, the fire is made ready, the furnace is now hot, ready to receive them; the flames do now rage and glow. The glittering sword is whet, and held over them, and the pit hath opened its mouth over them.

> Your wickedness makes you as it were heavy as lead, and to tend downwards with great weight and pressure towards hell; and if God should let you go, you would immediately sink and swiftly descend and plunge into the bottomless gulf.

> You cannot save yourself . . . your own care and . . . all your righteousness, would have no more influence to uphold you and keep you out of hell, than a spider's web would have to stop a fallen rock.

Real Life Says . . .

Edwards' "Sinners in the Hands of an Angry God" either repulses people in this world or shocks them. Many believe that God is too loving to condemn anyone; others believe that man is too good to be condemned. In fact, some have suggested that modern man is preaching his own sermon which could be entitled "*God* in the Hands of *Angry Sinners!*"

But the Bible is quite clear about the wrath of God. As we see in John 3:36, words from the Lord Jesus Himself, "Whoever believes in the Son has eternal life, but whoever rejects the Son will not see life, for God's wrath remains on him." Jeremiah 30:24 says, "The fierce anger of the LORD will not turn back until he fully accomplishes the purposes of his heart." As we will see in tomorrow's devotional, God's desire is not wrath, but rescue.

But, Lord . . .

Father, cause me to appreciate Your holy indignation against sin and to be thankful for Your Son taking the wrath I deserved upon Himself. In Jesus' name, Amen.

To Ponder . . .

It is sin not to be angry with sin. (Thomas Fuller)

Sinners in the Hands of an Angry God—Part 2

God's wrath is His "strange work." His desire is to pardon, rather than punish. But He must forgive on a righteous basis—and that is what the atoning work of Christ is all about.

Sin must be either pardoned or punished.

(Anonymous)

The vague and tenuous hope that God is too kind to punish the ungodly has become a deadly opiate for the consciences of millions.

(A.W. Tozer)

Who is a God like unto thee, that pardoneth iniquity, and passeth by the transgression of the remnant of his heritage? he retaineth not his anger for ever, because he delighteth in mercy.

(Micah 7:18, KJV)

The Knowledge Nugget

The philosopher Aristotle once said, "Anyone can become angry. That is easy. But to be angry with the right person, to the right degree, at the right time and in the right way—that is not easy." That seems to be an apt description of the anger—the wrath—of God. He is angry with the right person (all of humanity), to the right degree (His holiness and glory have been violated by man's sin), at the right time (God is "angry with the wicked every day," says Psalm 7:11, KJV), and in the right way (those who reject Christ, as we saw yesterday from John 3:36, still have the wrath of God "remaining" on them). God's anger is not haphazard; it is directed to all who have not been rescued from wrath by the atoning work of Christ. A brief glance at a concordance will show that God takes *wickedness* very seriously and will not compromise His holiness or His righteousness for any reason.

But Jesus declared that "God did not send his Son into the world to condemn the world, but to save the world through him" (John 3:17). God's heart desire is not to punish, but to pardon. Peter declared in his second epistle that God is "not wanting anyone to perish, but everyone to come to repentance" (2 Peter 3:9). The prophet Ezekiel declares *three times* that God takes no delight in the death of the wicked (18:23, 32; 33:11).

The only escape from God's judgment, declares the Lord Jesus Christ, is repentance and belief. But escape does not come without a price—the price paid by the Son of God. Jesus declared in anticipation of His death for man's sins, "Whoever believes in him is not condemned, but whoever does not believe stands condemned already because he has not believed in the name of God's one and only Son" (John 3:18). God's *desire* is not to condemn, but the only way one may be removed from God's ultimate condemnation is by believing in Jesus Christ. What about those who refuse to believe in Him? Jesus makes it quite clear that they stand condemned already. They are presently under the judgment of God.

Real Life Says . . .

As we saw in yesterday's devotional, many in our culture leave no room for God's wrath. Jonathan Edwards' sermon "Sinners in the

Hands of an Angry God" repulses them. There are even some evangelicals who accuse Edwards of being a sadist in concentrating so forcefully on God's judgment of hell. One professed evangelical, Clark Pinnock, writes, "Just as one can imagine certain people watching a cat trapped in a microwave oven squirming in agony and taking delight in it, so the saints in heaven will, according to Edwards, experience the torments of the damned with pleasure and satisfaction!"

R.C. Sproul responds, "A sadist who believed in hell would probably be more likely to give assurances to people that they were in no danger of hell, so he could deliciously relish the contemplation of their falling into it." A careful reading of Edwards' sermon shows his heart for the lost and his pleadings with them to turn from their sins and believe in Christ.

The prophet Micah declares: "Who is a God like unto thee, that pardoneth iniquity?" (7:18, KJV). But that pardon comes at the cost of God's one and only Son, the Lord Jesus Christ. Only He can turn away the righteous wrath of God.

But, Lord . . .

Father, I don't like to study the subject of Your holy wrath, but I need to. Remind me where I was spiritually before Your Son forgave my sins, so that I can speak to those who are still there. In Jesus' name, Amen.

To Ponder . . .

"For my own name's sake I delay my wrath." (Isaiah 48:9)

The Problem of Evil

The existence of evil and suffering in our world challenges the biblical doctrine of a God of love and justice. When the Christian seeks to speak of God's goodness and justice in this broken world, he is attempting to provide a *theodicy* (a word meaning a defense of God's justice in the face of evil's reality).

The skeptic Percy Bysshe Shelley wrote: "If God is the author of good, He is also the author of evil; if He is entitled to our gratitude for the one, He is entitled to our hatred for the other."

Whatever the answer to the problem of evil, this much is true: God took His own medicine.

(Dorothy Sayers)

Do you think that these Galileans were worse sinners than all the other Galileans because they suffered this way? I tell you, no! But unless you repent, you too will all perish.

(Luke 13:2-3)

The Knowledge Nugget

The doctrine of God's goodness has been under attack since Satan's challenge to Adam and Eve in the Garden of Eden. There he boldly denied God's goodness by declaring, "You will not surely die. . . . For God knows that when you eat of it [the tree of the knowledge of good and evil] your eyes will be opened, and you will be like God, knowing good and evil" (Genesis 3:4-5). His dis-information propaganda continues to this day.

A magazine called *The Secularist Humanist Bulletin* ridicules Christian belief in God's goodness. Laurence Perrine writes,

> Our God, some contend, is immutable,
> And their faith is, indeed, irrefutable;
> When He does what He should,
> It's because "He is good,"
> When He doesn't, "His ways are inscrutable."

Jesus dealt with the problem in evil in Luke 13 as He answered a question about the victims of Pilate's evil action (13:1-3). Pilate had massacred some Galilean believers while they were in the process of worshiping God. Jesus asks, "Do you think they were worse sinners than others in Galilee because they died this way? I tell you, no! But if you do not repent, you will likewise perish." Jesus Himself then refers to a tower in Siloam which fell on eighteen people, killing them. "Do you think they were worse sinners than all others in Jerusalem that they died this way? I tell you, no! But unless you repent, you too will all likewise perish" (13:4-5, author paraphrase).

In this important passage, Jesus deals with two major sources of suffering or evil in our world: vicious crimes (13:1-3) and violent accidents (13:4-5). Jesus' "theodicy" (His defense of God's justice in the face of evil's reality) emphasizes the brokenness and brevity of this life. Although He does not deal with all the philosophical questions raised about the problem of evil, He speaks powerfully to the question of tragedy in this world.

Real Life Says . . .

Our world desperately needs to hear the biblical answer to the problem of evil. God's Word teaches that this world is not the way God originally created it to be. There has been a real rebellion against God, and that rebellion has plunged all of creation into a fallen state. God allows evil and suffering to continue, part of the Christian answer declares, that men and women might see life's brevity and might get right with God.

Rabbi Harold Kushner's book *When Bad Things Happen to Good People* should be required reading for all Christians. Kushner does a fine job of shooting down many of the pat answers we Christians give to those that suffer, but his book has two major problems. The first problem is the title: there are no "good" people. The second problem is that Kushner's answer to the issue of evil is to compromise God's omnipotence (His all-powerfulness). He declares that he can far easier believe in a God who cannot intervene in suffering than in one who could intervene but chooses not to. In short, God is compassionate, but weak. The writer Ellie Wiesel rightly ridiculed Kushner's "answer" by saying, "If that's who God is, why doesn't He resign and let someone more competent take His place?"

But, Lord . . .

Father, we Christians seem to be under constant assault in this world. Thank You for Your complete competence to accomplish Your will in this world and in my life. In Jesus' name, Amen.

To Ponder . . .

God's competence and love should be judged primarily by what happened at Calvary.

The Problem of Pleasure

The Christian is often on the defensive because of the problem of evil. But what about the good things of life? Where do *they* come from? Christianity teaches that the God who exists gives good gifts as evidences of His love for His creation.

Concerned doctor with stethoscope on patient's chest: "You've been enjoying something again!"

(Joe Mirachi)

Puritanism is the haunting fear that someone, somewhere, may be happy.

(H.L. Mencken)

Command those who are rich in this present world not to be arrogant nor to put their hope in wealth, which is so uncertain, but to put their hope in God, who richly provides us with everything for our enjoyment.

(1 Timothy 6:17)

The Knowledge Nugget

Steve Brown tells about a recent experiment conducted with rats and two buttons. If the rats pushed one of the buttons, food would come down a little trough and they would be fed. The other button, wired to the pleasure center of their brain, when pushed would deliver a little jolt

Great Is the God We Adore .... DAY TWENTY-ONE

of electricity that was extremely pleasurable. The scientists found that without a single exception, those rats pushed the pleasure button every time. Only the pleasure button. Time after time. Until they starved to death.

Christians have struggled with the issue of pleasure throughout church history. Some (the libertarians) argued that because we are free in Christ, even unbiblical pleasures can be enjoyed, for the Christian can confess sin, find forgiveness with God and continue to live as he chooses. It is no wonder that the Apostle Paul had to write to the Roman believers, "What shall we say then? Shall we go on sinning that grace may increase? By no means! We died to sin; how can we live in it any longer?" (Romans 6:1-2).

Other Christians (the ascetics) argued that the body is the prison house of the soul, and so physical pleasures should be shunned, even to the extent of turning away from food, clothing and shelter. (Remember the devotional on Simeon Stylites on Day 11 of Section One?) But C.S. Lewis reminds us in his book *Mere Christianity* that:

> There is no good trying to be more spiritual than God. God never meant man to be a purely spiritual creature. That is why He uses material things like bread and wine to put the new life into us. We may think this rather crude and unspiritual. God does not: He invented eating. He likes matter. He invented it.

The Bible takes the middle road between libertarianism and asceticism, setting forth the pleasures of life as gifts of God. Denying the gnostic view that the material world is evil, the Bible says that the Creator God was pleased with His creation, and that He is the God who finds joy in His people (Psalm 147:11).

Real Life Says . . .

What a twisted view of God and His creation many people have today! They criticize God for the evil things they observe, but refuse to give

Him "credit" for His good gifts. In his essay "The Problem of Pleasure," Philip Yancey reminds us that pleasures such as colors, taste and music are all gifts of a good God. And the unbeliever is hard-pressed to explain such joys in life. Again Lewis (in his *Mere Christianity*) corrects the Christian:

> I know some muddle-headed Christians have talked as if Christianity thought that sex, or the body, or pleasure, were bad in themselves. But they were wrong. Christianity is almost the only one of the great religions which thoroughly approves of the body—which believes that matter is good, that God Himself once took on a human body, that some kind of body is going to be given to us even in Heaven and is going to be an essential part of our happiness, our beauty and our energy. Christianity has glorified marriage more than any other religion: and nearly all the greatest love poetry in the world has been produced by Christians.

Paul reminds us, "Command those who are rich in this present world not to be arrogant nor to put their hope in wealth, which is so uncertain, but to put their hope in God, who richly provides us with everything for our enjoyment" (1 Timothy 6:17).

But, Lord . . .

Father, please give me a biblical balance on this issue of pleasure, that I might praise You for Your good gifts. In Jesus' name, Amen.

To Ponder . . .

We belong to a God at whose "right hand there are pleasures for evermore" (Psalm 16:11, KJV).

As Good As His Word

When we speak of the integrity of God, we mean that He cannot lie. He speaks only the truth.

Integrity is not a conditional word. It doesn't blow in the wind or change with the weather. It is your inner image of yourself, and if you look in there and see a man who won't cheat, then you know he never will.

(John D. MacDonald)

Apart from blunt truth, our lives sink decadently amid the perfume of hints and suggestions.

(Anonymous)

It is impossible for God to lie.

(Hebrews 6:18)

The Knowledge Nugget

A golfer was on the practice tee when the club pro, Maury, brought an important-looking man out for a lesson. Maury watched the guy swing several times and started making suggestions for improvement, but each time the pupil interrupted with his own version of what was wrong and how to correct it. After a few minutes of this interference, Maury began nodding his head in agreement. At the end of the lesson, the man paid Maury, congratulated him on his expertise as a teacher and left in an obviously pleased frame of mind.

The observer was so astonished by the performance that he had to ask the golf pro, "Why did you put up with him?"

"Son," the old pro said with a grin as he carefully pocketed his fee, "I learned long ago that it's a waste of time to sell answers to a man who wants to buy echoes."

The God of the Bible does not sell echoes. He tells the truth. Only the truth. Always. The Bible challenges the believer to "buy the truth and do not sell it" (Proverbs 23:23). And truth is all that God is "selling."

When we speak of God as a God of truth, we mean that He is the only true God (Jeremiah 10:10; John 17:3) who acts and speaks in a perfectly consistent way with His own nature. God is what He appears to be. A vice-president for public affairs at a Christian college used to define public relations as "nine-tenths being what you say you are, and one-tenth modestly saying it." God is not only nine-tenths true; He is ten-tenths true!

We use the term *veracity* when we speak of God's truthfulness. He represents things as they really are. There is no "spin" with God; He does not exaggerate, embellish or cover up the truth. God's attribute of omniscience guarantees that no information escapes His notice. He cannot deceive or lie, the writer to the Hebrews tells us (6:18). God's inability to speak anything other than the truth is a virtue, not a vice, for He cannot be or do anything inconsistent with His own nature.

Real Life Says . . .

The biblical doctrine of God's integrity, veracity and truthfulness permeates all of Scripture. Someone has said that "Since God is truth, a contempt for truth is equally a contempt for God." If Jesus was telling the truth when He said that "men loved darkness instead of light because their deeds were evil" (John 3:19)—*and He was*—the Christian should not be surprised that a thoroughly truthful God is not a welcome thought to many people today.

But the world needs to hear of our God who is as good as His Word. A man used to visit his music teacher friend and asked him rather flippantly, "What's the good news today?" The old man picked up a tuning fork and struck it lightly with a small hammer. As the note sounded throughout the room, he said, "That is the note 'A.' It is 'A' today; it was 'A' five thousand years ago, and it will be 'A' ten thousand years from now. The soprano upstairs sings off-key, the tenor across the hall becomes flat on his high notes, and the piano downstairs is out of tune." He struck the note again. "But that is 'A,' my friend, and that's the good news for today."

But, Lord . . .

Father, I need Your truth more than I realize. Thank You that You love me enough to tell me the truth and to deliver it with Your love. In Jesus' name, Amen.

To Ponder . . .

"I, the LORD, speak the truth; I declare what is right" (Isaiah 45:19).

The names of God reveal His character and show His concern for His creation. Studying the many names of God as set forth in Scripture tells us much about His attributes.

Humorist Weare Holbrook once said, "I am all in favor of name-dropping—names are the raisins in the rice pudding of conversation."

A name is made up of little promises kept to the letter. It is made up of faithfulness, loyalty, honesty, of efficiency in your work. In short, a name is the blueprint of the thing we call character. You ask, "What's in a name?" I answer, "Just about everything you do."

(Morris Mandel)

Moses said to God, "Suppose I go to the Israelites and say to them, 'The God of your fathers has sent me to you,' and they ask me, 'What is his name?' Then what shall I tell them?"

God said to Moses, "I AM WHO I AM. This is what you are to say to the Israelites: 'I AM has sent me to you.' "

God also said to Moses, "Say to the Israelites, 'The LORD, the God of your fathers—the God of Abraham, the God of Isaac and the God of Jacob—has sent me to you.' This is my name forever, the name by which I am to be remembered from generation to generation."

(Exodus 3:13-15)

The Knowledge Nugget

In a delightful and thought-provoking book entitled *Wishful Thinking: A Theological ABC*, Frederick Buechner defines various theological and religious terms. He defines words like "heaven," "anger" and "devil." Under the "B's," he even has the following entry:

> BUECHNER: It is my name. It is pronounced Beekner. If somebody mispronounces it in some foolish way, I have the feeling that what's foolish is me. If somebody forgets it, I feel that it's I who am forgotten. There's something about it that embarrasses me in just the same way that there's something about me that embarrasses me. I can't imagine myself with any other name—Held, say, or Merrill, or Hlavacek. If my name were different, I would be different. When I tell somebody my name, I have given him a hold over me that he didn't have before. If he calls it out, I stop, look, and listen whether I want to or not. In the Book of Exodus, God tells Moses that his name is Yahweh, and God hasn't had a peaceful moment since.

The Scriptures are filled with the names of God. Each of His "hyphenated" names—Jehovah-jireh (Genesis 22), Jehovah-nissi (Exodus 17) and Jehovah-shalom (Judges 6)—are worth studying in its context, for each illustrates how God meets the deepest needs of His people.

The psalms are filled with an enthusiasm about the name of God. "O LORD, our Lord, how majestic is your name in all the earth!" (Psalm 8:1). "We give thanks to you, O God, we give thanks, for your Name is near; men tell of your wonderful deeds" (75:1). The Psalmist often speaks of "fearing" God's name (see 61:5; 102:15). For example, he prays, "Teach me your way, O LORD, and I will walk in your truth; give me an undivided heart, that I may fear your name" (86:11).

Real Life Says . . .

The contemporary "theologian" Oprah Winfrey once mocked the idea of God having a specific name and being jealous when He is not worshiped. She said, "'IT' doesn't *care* what we call 'IT'!" But her New Age spirituality is a far cry from the biblical revelation of the true God.

A writer named Russler Luthi reminds us:

> God has a name. The misery on the earth is nameless; the evil among men is nameless, for the powers of darkness love to be without a name. . . . Anonymous letters, letters without signatures are usually vulgar. But God is no writer of anonymous letters. God puts His name on everything that He does, affects, and says. . . . When God entered time and space, we learned about love and we learned His name. "And she will bring forth a Son, and you shall call His name Jesus, for He will save His people from their sins."

But, Lord . . .

Father, I praise You for Your names. Help me today to bear Your name before a world that needs you. In Jesus' name, Amen.

To Ponder . . .

God wants to communicate His names because He wants us to know Him.

Despising God

When we ignore God's Word, we are showing disdain for God Himself.

If I thought there was an omnipotent God who looked down on battles and death and all the waste and horror of this war [World War I]—able to prevent these things—doing them to amuse Himself, I would spit in His empty face.

(H.G. Wells)

Every time we sin, we are doing something that God hates. . . . We become so accustomed to our sins we sometimes lapse into a state of peaceful coexistence with them, but God never ceases to hate them.

(Jerry Bridges)

Why did you *despise the word of the LORD* by doing what is evil in his eyes? You struck down Uriah the Hittite with the sword and took his wife to be your own. . . . Now, therefore, the sword will never depart from your house, because *you despised me* and took the wife of Uriah the Hittite to be your own.

(2 Samuel 12:9-10, emphasis added)

The Knowledge Nugget

After the Bob Harrington/Madeline Murray O'Hare debates several years ago, O'Hare expressed her beliefs about Christianity:

> Christianity is intolerant, anti-democratic, anti-sexual, and anti-life. It is anti-woman and I cannot stand that. It is anti-everything that is good and human and decent and kind and love-filled and understanding. I used to have an intellectual hatred for Christianity. I think that is broadening now. I am *enjoying* hating the whole thing.

When she vanished some years later, O'Hare was thought to have been murdered. One can only hope that she changed her mind about the person of Christ before death came.

H.G. Wells, a brilliant author (*War of the Worlds*, *The Invisible Man*) and humorist, once left a Cambridge party, accidentally picking up a hat that did not belong to him. Discovering his mistake, he decided not to return the headgear to its rightful owner, whose label was inside the brim. The hat fit Wells comfortably; furthermore, he had grown to like it. So he wrote to the former owner: "I stole your hat; I like your hat; I shall keep your hat. Whenever I look inside it I shall think of you and your excellent sherry and of the town of Cambridge. I take off your hat to you."

But Wells, like O'Hare, expressed an indifference and, at times, a hatred for Christianity. His statement about World War I makes sense, for the biblical God is no sadist. But such examples of pure hatred for Christianity and for the God of Christians should not surprise us. What *should* surprise us is what took place in Second Samuel, chapters 11-12.

Those two chapters describe the moral collapse of David, the king of Israel, the "sweet psalmist." He saw a woman he wanted, took her, got her pregnant, then tried to get her husband to come home from the battlefield and sleep with his wife (so everyone would think that Bathsheba's pregnancy was Uriah's doing). King David even got this godly warrior drunk, hoping that he would give in and spend some

"R&R" at home. When he steadfastly refused to forsake his military duties, David had Uriah murdered by ordering Israel's commander Joab to abandon this brave soldier on the battlefield.

Real Life Says . . .

Many in this world say that you should go after what you want, that you don't need to consider the consequences of your actions and by all means don't let your desires be hampered by what God's Word says. But King David is rebuked by Nathan the prophet in Second Samuel 12 for his lust, his failure to guard the children of Israel and his abuse of his power in taking what he wanted.

As the focus of his rebuke, Nathan says to David on behalf of the Lord, "Why did you *despise the word of the LORD* by doing what is evil in his eyes? You struck down Uriah the Hittite with the sword and took his wife to be your own. . . . Now, therefore, the sword will never depart from your house, because *you despised me* and took the wife of Uriah the Hittite to be your own" (12:9-10, emphasis added). Despising God's Word equals despising God Himself!

But, Lord . . .

Father, I would never say that I hated You! Help me to realize that willful disobedience to Your Word is the same as despising You. In Jesus' name, Amen.

To Ponder . . .

God is affected by the way we treat His Word. It matters to Him when we sin.

God and Time

The Bible teaches that there was never a time when God did not exist. His existence is not derived from anything external to Himself. God does not grow or develop, for He is always the same: perfect in knowledge, in love and in Himself. He is never taken by surprise nor does He ever need to come up with contingency plans. But He is conscious of the succession of points of time with us.

The center of me is always and eternally a terrible pain—a curious wild pain—a searching for something beyond what the world contains.

(Bertrand Russell)

All that is not eternal is eternally out of date.

(C.S. Lewis)

He has made everything beautiful in its time. He has also set eternity in the hearts of men; yet they cannot fathom what God has done from beginning to end.

(Ecclesiastes 3:11)

The Knowledge Nugget

Several of my friends do a great deal of international traveling. They tell of leaving the States and going across the world, and losing a whole day because of the various time zones they pass through. Conversely, they talk about leaving from some country in Asia and returning home the same day even though they have been flying for a full day. It makes one wonder: Does God ever get jet lag?

When we study the issue of God and time, we need to be reminded of the doctrine of God's infinity, a theological term meaning that God is unlimited and unlimitable. He is unlimited and unlimitable in regard to space. We use the term "omnipresence" to indicate, as one theologian puts it, "wherever there's a where, God is there." But He is also unlimited and unlimitable in terms of knowledge. The term "omniscience" indicates that God knows everything. He never needs to be informed about something; He never grows in His understanding; He does not "gather facts" (although certain biblical passages describe God in human language which seems to indicate the processing of information, such as Genesis 11:5-6).

When we speak of God being unlimited and unlimitable in regard to time, the term "infinity" or "eternity" or "eternality" is used. The author Tennessee Williams once said that "Snatching the eternal out of the desperately fleeting is the great magic trick of human existence." God does not need to do any "snatching," for He stands eternally outside of, above and in control of time.

Real Life Says . . .

For many in our world the question of God's relation to time has never occurred to them. Few seem to realize that "how we spend our days," as Annie Dillard said, "is, of course, how we spend our lives." And our lives are meant to be spent serving the eternal God.

Certain time words are used of the Lord throughout Scripture. For example, the psalmist declares: "Lord, you have been our dwelling place throughout all *generations*. Before the mountains were *born* or you brought forth the earth and the world, *from everlasting to everlasting* you are God" (Psalm 90:1-2, emphasis added). The true God is not generation-bound. He does not belong to or care only about one generation. And His being precedes the creation of the mountains, the earth and the world. Although words fail us here, from "eternity past" to "eternity future," He is God!

But the psalmist is not done. He contrasts this eternal God with finite man: "You turn men back to dust, saying, 'Return to dust, O sons of men.' For a thousand years in your sight are like a day that has just gone by, or like a watch in the night. You sweep men away in the sleep of death; they are like the new grass of the morning—though in the morning it springs up new, by evening it is dry and withered" (90:3-6).

To belong to this God of eternity is man's greatest blessing. To be used by Him at this present moment of history is an individual's highest calling.

But, Lord . . .

Father of eternity, I praise You for the fact that You are in control of time. Help me today to use my moments to glorify Christ. In Jesus' name, Amen.

To Ponder . . .

The humans live in time, but our Enemy [God] destines them to eternity. He therefore, I believe, wants them to attend chiefly to two things, to eternity itself and to that point of time which they call the Present. For the Present is the point at which time touches eternity. (C.S. Lewis, *Screwtape Letters*)

The Worth of Worship

Worship is the redeemed heart's response to the person and work of God. It is acknowledging His grace, His character and His lovingkindness to His children.

Our problem today is that we worship our work, work at our play, and play at our worship.

(Gordon Dahl)

So long as man remains free he strives for nothing so incessantly and so painfully as to find someone to worship.

(Fyodor Dostoyevsky)

Ascribe to the LORD, O mighty ones,
   ascribe to the LORD glory and strength.
Ascribe to the LORD the glory due his name;
   worship the LORD in the splendor of his holiness.

(Psalm 29:1-2)

The Knowledge Nugget

Henry Norris Russell, a Princeton astronomer, had just concluded a lecture on the Milky Way when a woman came to him and asked, "If our world is so little, and the universe is so great, how can we believe that God pays any attention to us?"

DAY TWENTY-SIX .... *Great Is the God We Adore*

Dr. Russell replied, "That depends, madam, entirely on how big a God you believe in."

Our God is so big that He pays attention to every detail of our lives. The question is, do we pay attention to Him?

The Bible declares that God is a "jealous God." "There is no need to be disturbed by this," says John Stott. "Jealousy is a resentment of rivals, and whether it is good or evil depends on whether the rival has any right to be there. Since God is unique, and there is no other, he has the right to ask that we worship him alone." As we saw in our devotional on "The Idiocy of Idolatry" (Day 13 of this section), God ridicules the creation and worship of idols for they can't hear, speak, see, smell or help (Psalm 115:5-7).

In contrast to idols the true God hears His people's prayers, speaks His truth into their lives, sees their needs, smells their fragrant offerings of prayer and helps those whom He loves. The highest calling for the Christian is to get to know his God, for, as Earl Radmacher rightly says, "An unknown God can neither be trusted nor worshiped." The pursuit of theology must be the pursuit of a deeper knowledge of the living and true God. And that study must not become a pool of information which is hoarded to oneself; it should be shared with others and be used to mature our own worship of the Lord.

Real Life Says . . .

The very concept of worship is a foreign one to many today. Perhaps it is because they have observed the frequently anemic rituals of Christians which seem to possess so little life and vitality and excitement about God.

In John 4 Jesus had a fascinating theological discussion with an outcast Samaritan woman. The Samaritans and the orthodox Jews avoided each other like the plague, and Jesus aroused her attention when He spoke to her, asking her for water. He responded to her puzzlement with a cryptic statement: "If you knew the gift of God and who it is that asks you for a drink, you would have asked him and he would have given you living water" (4:10). That "living water," Jesus said, would become in the person who receives it a "spring of water welling up to eternal life" (4:14). Before He was able to give her this water, Jesus needed to deal with her sin. And He lovingly confronted her with her immoral lifestyle (she had been with six men in her life). His personal insight into her life convinced her that He was a prophet, and she then engaged Jesus in a theological discussion about *where* one ought to worship God. Jesus redirected the conversation away from the question of geography to the issue of the *heart*: "Believe me, woman, a time is coming when you will worship the Father neither on this mountain nor in Jerusalem. . . . A time is coming and has now come when the true worshipers will worship the Father in spirit and in truth, for they are the kind of worshipers the Father seeks" (4:21, 23). He is still seeking those kind of worshipers.

But, Lord . . .

Father, I am so often so weak in my worship. Mature me in my faith that I might worship You in spirit and in truth. In Jesus' name, Amen.

To Ponder . . .

When Christian worship is dull and joyless, Jesus Christ has been left outside—that is the only possible explanation. (James Stewart)

We please God not only when we worship Him, praising Him for His goodness, mercy and love, but also when we submit our lives to Him to be used for His glory.

What is the chief end [purpose] of man? To glorify God and to enjoy Him forever.

(*The Westminster Shorter Catechism*)

Though Christ can be grieved at a thousand things in us that no eye but His can see, yet none [is] so easily pleased as He by our little endeavors of love.

(R.C. Chapman)

So we make it our goal to please him, whether we are at home in the body or away from it.

(2 Corinthians 5:9)

The Knowledge Nugget

As we discussed in an earlier devotional, the creeds and confessions developed by Christians are often helpful in summarizing the key doctrines of the Christian faith. I am so thankful that those who were used by God to pen what is called *The Westminster Shorter Catechism* gave both a biblical and a comprehensive answer to the question, "What is the chief end [purpose] of man?" They could have simply said, "To worship Him with all of one's heart, soul, mind and strength," which would have been biblical, but incomplete. Instead they gave a twofold answer: "The chief purpose of man is to glorify God *and to enjoy Him forever.*"

The real question is not do we enjoy God, but does He ever enjoy *us?* Is He a God who takes pleasure in *us?* It is one thing to completely submit to and serve an almighty potentate who will strike down those who do not bow before Him. It is quite another thing to realize that we belong to a loving God who can be pleased by His people.

Although somewhat lengthy, J.C. Ryle speaks powerfully about the Christian in regard to this question of pleasing God:

> [The Christian] only sees one thing, he cares for one thing, he lives for one thing, he is swallowed up in one thing; and that one thing is to please God. Whether he lives, or whether he dies—whether he has health, or whether he has sickness—whether he is rich, or whether he is poor—whether he pleases man, or whether he gives offence—whether he is thought wise, or whether he is thought foolish—whether he gets blame, or whether he gets praise—whether he gets honor, or whether he gets shame—for all this the zealous man cares nothing at all. He burns for one thing: and that one thing is to please God, and to advance God's glory. If he is consumed in the very burning, he cares not for it—he is content. He feels that, like a lamp, he is made to burn; and if consumed in burning, he has but done the work for which God appointed him. Such a one will always find a sphere for his zeal. If he cannot preach, work, and give money, he will cry, and sigh, and pray. . . . If he cannot fight in the valley with Joshua, he will do the work of Moses, Aaron, and Hur, on the hill (Exodus 17:9-13). If he is cut off from

working himself, he will give the Lord no rest till help is raised up from another quarter, and the work is done.

Real Life Says . . .

On this issue of pleasing God, many today think that God doesn't care how people live, or they conceive of God as a selfish, self-centered dictator who, like the capricious Greek gods, insists upon unending adoration.

The biblical doctrine of the true God is that He is perfect, infinite, loving and merciful. When people worship Him, they are coming into contact with reality itself. We were meant to worship God, and when we do we are by that practice becoming more fully ourselves. True joy is found only in living life to please Him.

But, Lord . . .

Father, I have only begun to scratch the surface of what it means to please You. Thank You that You are pleased by the praises of Your people. In Jesus' name, Amen.

To Ponder . . .

"His pleasure is not in the strength of the horse, nor his delight in the legs of a man; the LORD delights in those who fear him, who put their hope in his unfailing love." (Psalm 147:10-11)

The Providence of God

Today's Focus

Defined as God's continuing care of His creation, providence involves God preserving His world and guiding it to His intended purposes. This doctrine reminds us that God is active and present in our lives.

Sometimes I think we're alone in the universe, and sometimes I think we're not. In either case, the idea is quite staggering.

(Arthur C. Clarke)

Now if I believe in God's Son and bear in mind that He became man, all creatures will appear a hundred times more beautiful to me than before. Then I will properly appreciate the sun, the moon, the stars, trees, apples, pears, as I reflect that He is Lord over and the center of all things.

(Martin Luther)

The LORD is good to all;
   he has compassion on all he has made. . . .
The eyes of all look to you,
   and you give them their food at the proper time.
You open your hand
   and satisfy the desires of every living thing.

(Psalm 145:9, 15-16)

The Knowledge Nugget

A little girl had accompanied her mother to the country store where, after the mother had made a purchase, the clerk invited the child to help herself to a handful of candy. The youngster held back. "What's the matter? Don't you like candy?" asked the clerk. The child nodded, and smilingly the clerk put his hand into the jar and dropped a generous portion into the little girl's handbag. Afterward the mother asked her daughter why she had not taken the candy when the clerk first offered some to her. She replied, "Because his hand is bigger than mine!"

God's hands are the biggest of all—and we forget His generous provisions for us. The doctrine of providence reminds us that the Creator cares about His creation, sustaining and guiding it to His intended purposes.

During the early years of this country's founding, individuals like Thomas Jefferson held to a religious viewpoint known as deism, which suggested that the world was made by a God who is now distant and uninvolved. He wound up the universe like a watch and now it ticks on its own.

Biblical Christianity teaches that God is intimately involved in every aspect of His creation. David writes,

> You care for the land and water it;
>   you enrich it abundantly.
> The streams of God are filled with water
>   to provide the people with grain,
>   for so you have ordained it.
> You drench its furrows
>   and level its ridges;
> you soften it with showers
>   and bless its crops.
> You crown the year with your bounty,
>   and your carts overflow with abundance.
> The grasslands of the desert overflow;
>   the hills are clothed with gladness.
> The meadows are covered with flocks

and the valleys are mantled with grain;
they shout for joy and sing. (Psalm 65:9-13)

Note the verbs used by the psalmist to show God's active management of His world: "You care for . . . water . . . enrich" and "provide the people with grain." Lest someone conclude that only the "laws of nature" are in operation, the psalmist says that God has "ordained" the cycle of water for the crops to grow. His exuberant care is shown by words like "bounty," "your carts overflow with abundance" and "the grasslands of the desert [!] overflow." And the writer describes the meadows and the valleys as shouting for joy and singing!

Real Life Says . . .

Rather than accepting the biblical doctrine of God's providence, the world chooses to believe either that there is no Creator/Sustainer (the theory of evolution) or that the Creation itself is to be worshiped (the idea of "Mother Nature" or the "gaia" concept found in New Age thinking). How sad to miss the true God's watch-care over His world!

God "has not left himself without testimony," says the Apostle Paul. "He has shown kindness by giving you rain from heaven and crops in their seasons; he provides you with plenty of food and fills your hearts with joy" (Acts 14:17). Such gifts from God's open hand ought to bring us to our senses and lead us to praise Him!

But, Lord . . .

Father, thank You for caring for Your creation, including me! Help me to trust You and Your plans for my life. In Jesus' name, Amen.

To Ponder . . .

"He who did not spare his own Son, but gave him up for us all—how will he not also, along with him, graciously give us all things?" (Romans 8:32)

Removing God's Anonymity

The follower of Jesus Christ, the "Christian," bears God's name. And our task in this world is to make known the unknown God.

To the Editor:
I'm writing this letter,
Quite frankly, to say
I abhorred the column
You wrote yesterday!
It was weak and insipid
And words synonymous—
In short, it lacked courage!
Yours truly, Anonymous.

(Mary Grace Dembeck)

The disciples were called Christians first at Antioch.

(Acts 11:26)

Men of Athens! I see that in every way you are very religious. For as I walked around and looked carefully at your objects of worship, I even found an altar with this inscription: TO AN UNKNOWN GOD. Now what you worship as something unknown I am going to proclaim to you.

(17:22-23)

The Knowledge Nugget

The story is told of a television reporter in New York who had a terrible time pronouncing names. While he was on the air, someone handed him a note that said that the prime minister of South Africa, Heinrich VerVoot, had been killed. The reporter looked down at this awful name and said, "The prime minister of South Africa has just been killed." After a long pause, he said, "And we are withholding the name pending the notification of the relatives."

God does not withhold His name, but, as we have seen in this section's Day 23 devotional, the believer in Jesus Christ is to spread His name abroad and proclaim His actions among the children of men!

Rather than being an abstract force or impersonal power, the living God discloses His personality through His names. The psalmist declares, "Some trust in chariots and some in horses, but we trust in the name of the LORD our God" (Psalm 20:7). David issues an invitation to all who know the Lord: "O magnify the LORD with me, and let us exalt his name together" (34:3, KJV).

When I was young my grandmother lived with us. She was a gentle soul who could bake the best marble cake you've ever tasted! But what I really appreciated about her was that she would let me borrow her magnifying glass from her dresser. I used that magnifying glass to burn the initials of high school girlfriends on my goalpost (there really weren't that many) and to start small fires in our backyard. But I didn't use her magnifying glass for what it was intended: *to make larger, to magnify*! That's what we believers are to do with the name of God! Again, it is the psalmist who says, "I will praise the name of God with a song, and will magnify him with thanksgiving" (69:30, KJV).

Real Life Says . . .

Our world is not comfortable with the names of God, because a named god is a specific god. Many are much happier with a variety of nameless deities. But the Christian has become very specific about identifying the real God—and spreading His name from shore to shore! Why is the Christian under compulsion to remove God's anonymity from the world? The answer is quite simple: *He alone is God and all other gods are imposters.* He alone can grant salvation, the psalmist declares: "He provided redemption for his people; he ordained his covenant forever—holy and awesome is his name" (111:9).

And the God of the Bible is no tribal deity, confined to one people or one country. Again the psalmist declares:

> Shout with joy to God, all the earth!
> Sing the glory of his name;
> make his praise glorious!
> Say to God, "How awesome are your deeds!
> So great is your power
> that your enemies cringe before you.
> All the earth bows down to you;
> they sing praise to you,
> they sing praise to your name." (66:1-4)

The Christian's task is to invite others to join that choir! Because we have been created in the image of God, and because we were designed to praise Him for His marvelous deeds, then proclaiming His name is not a task, but a privilege!

But, Lord . . .

Father, I know that an unknown god can neither be trusted nor worshiped. And You have decided to use me to make You known to this needy world. Thank You for the part I can play in making Your name known. In Jesus' name, Amen.

To Ponder . . .

Why is it important that you identify yourself as a Christian? So that those who want to be introduced to God will know who to go to. (Steve Brown)

Seeing God
Face-to-Face

The Bible teaches that the believer in Christ will one day see the Lord "face to face." What some theologians called the "beatific vision" is, indeed, the Christian's hope and goal.

The face is the index of the mind.

(Latin proverb)

Though Christians believe in heaven, sometimes they act as though going there were a calamity.

(Henry Jacobsen)

Now we see but a poor reflection as in a mirror; then we shall see face to face. Now I know in part; then I shall know fully, even as I am fully known.

(1 Corinthians 13:12)

The Knowledge Nugget

Mark Twain once quipped, "You take heaven. I'd rather go to Bermuda." His sentiment does not seem that far off the mark in describing many Christians' lack of enthusiasm for what they term "going home to be with the Lord." We are like the little boy in Sunday school who listened intently while the teacher told about the beauties of heaven. She concluded by saying, "All who are glad you are going to heaven raise your hands." Every hand shot up immediately—except one. "Why don't you want to go to heaven, Johnny?" "Well," he replied, "when I left home, Mom was baking an apple pie."

The pleasures of this life are to be enjoyed, but they can easily become a substitute for the believer's ultimate destiny, which is to be with the Lord forever. What will be involved in "going to heaven"? The Bible has much to say about the believer's ultimate home. But one thing is certain: we will see the Lord "face-to-face."

When the Apostle Paul uses those words in First Corinthians 13:12 ("Now we see but a poor reflection as in a mirror; then we shall see face to face. Now I know in part; then I shall know fully, even as I am fully known"), we are reminded of several other passages of Scriptures in which individuals believed they saw God "face-to-face."

Jacob wrestled with an angel in order to receive the blessing of God in Genesis 32. He named the place of his wrestling match "Peniel," a term meaning "face of God," and said, "It is because I saw God face to face, and yet my life was spared." (Genesis 32:30).

Moses is described as the "friend of God" because of his frequent conversations with the Almighty. Exodus 33 tells us: "The LORD would speak to Moses face to face, as a man speaks with his friend" (33:11). On one occasion, God threatened to destroy His unbelieving people Israel, promising to start over with Moses.

> Moses said to the LORD, "Then the Egyptians will hear about it! By your power you brought these people up from among them. And they will tell the inhabitants of this land about it. They have already heard that you, O LORD, are with these people and that you, O LORD, have been seen face to face, that your cloud stays over them, and that you go before them in a pillar of cloud by day and a pillar of fire by night. If you put these people to death all at one time, the nations who have heard this report about you will say, 'The LORD was not able to bring these people into the land

he promised them on oath; so he slaughtered them in the desert.'" (Numbers 14:13-16)

Moses feared that God's power would be questioned if He acted in deserved judgment against His people.

Real Life Says . . .

In this section's Day 14 devotional, we noted the statement by Jean-Paul Sartre, the famous existentialist philosopher, who said, "The last thing I want is to be subject to the unremitting gaze of a holy God." But for those who have been "washed in the blood of the Lamb," they look forward to gazing upon the One whose love rescued them from their sins. And that desire will be granted (1 Corinthians 13:12)!

But, Lord . . .

Father, continue to deepen my love for You so that the prospect of seeing You face-to-face will be my daily joy. In Jesus' name, Amen.

To Ponder . . .

"Anyone who has seen me has seen the Father." (John 14:9)

Glossary of Terms

agnostic: One who says he does not know whether there is a God. *Section 3, Day 3/4*

allegorize: To interpret a section of the Bible symbolically; to go beyond the plain or simple meaning of a text. *Section 2, Day 22*

apologetic: A word meaning "defense." *Section 1, Day 17*

asceticism: A philosophy which emphasizes the turning away from the basic of human pleasures. *Section 1, Day 11; Section 3, Day 21*

ascetics: Christians who have argued that the body is the prison house of the soul and so even basic human needs should be shunned. *Section 3, Day 21*

atheist: One who declares there is no God. *Section 3, Day 3*

attribute: A characteristic of God's person or nature. *Section 1, Day 12*

authority: The right to determine what one believes or how one behaves. *Section 2, Day 1*

autonomy: Man's being a law unto himself. *Section 2, Day 4*

beatific vision: The Christian's hope of seeing God face-to-face. *Section 3, Day 30*

"Berean believer": A Christian who tests what he hears with what the Bible teaches. *Section 2, Day 5*

canon: A word originally meaning "rule" or "measure." Refers to the accepted collection of inspired books that make up the Bible. *Section 2, Day 12*

confession:	Synonymous with the term "creed"; a brief statement of some key truths of biblical faith. *Section 1, Day 13*
context:	The surrounding verses of a text that must be studied so that the correct understanding will be achieved. *Section 2, Day 18*
creed:	A brief statement of some key truths of biblical faith. *Section 1, Day 13*
deism:	The belief that God created the universe, but God is now distant and uninvolved. *Section 3, Day 28*
distinctive:	A belief or opinion held by Christians which is not mandated by the Word of God. *Section 1, Day 18*
Docetism:	A worldview in the first few centuries of the Christian Church which cast doubt on the genuine humanity of Christ. *Section 1, Day 9*
doubt:	A position that opens one up to the possibility of either belief or unbelief. *Section 1, Day 23*
essential:	A belief which is clearly taught in the Word of God. *Section 1, Day 18*
eternity of God:	God is unlimited and unlimitable in regard to time. *Section 3, Day 25*
exclusion:	The concept that some books which claim to be of God did not make their way into the canon of Scripture. *Section 2, Day 12*
existentialism:	A philosophy that emphasizes the uniqueness of individual existence in a hostile universe. *Section 1, Day 15*
faith:	May refer to one's confidence in God or to the content of truth God has given. *Section 1, Day 1*
freedom:	Not the right to do what one wants, but the power to do what one should. *Section 2, Day 29*

general revelation:	God's communication of some of His truths to all people everywhere through creation, human nature and history. *Section 2, Day 13*
gnosticism:	A movement which said that Jesus gave some secret teachings to those who were not apostles and that the early Christians' faith was incomplete without this new knowledge. *Section 1, Day 9*
grace:	God's undeserved favor. *Section 3, Day 10/11*
heresy:	A term meaning choice or division or faction. *Section 1, Day 8*
historical theology:	The study of how doctrines have been understood since the church was founded. *Section 1, Day 11*
holiness:	God's personal and active righteousness. *Section 3, Day 14/15*
holy rage:	An anguish at the destructive power of sin. *Section 2, Day 28*
idolatry:	The worshiping of any created object, including the thoughts of man. *Section 3, Day 13*
illumination:	The ministry of the Holy Spirit by which He opens our minds to the truth and application of the Word of God. *Section 2, Day 25*
inclusion:	The concept that no books which are truly of God have been left out of our Bibles. *Section 2, Day 12*
inerrancy:	What was written in the Scriptures is not liable to be proven false or mistaken. *Section 2, Day 15/24*
infallibility:	The belief that the Scriptures are incapable of teaching deception. *Section 2, Day 15*
infinity:	God is unlimited and unlimitable in regard to time. *Section 3, Day 25*

inspiration:	The "out-breathing" of God's truth through His chosen and protected instruments. *Section 2, Day 15*
integrity:	God cannot lie; He speaks only the truth. *Section 3, Day 22*
jealousy:	A resentment of rivals; God's demand that we worship Him alone, for only He is worthy of our worship. *Section 3, Day 26*
liberal theology:	Theology which denies the fundamental truths or doctrines of the Word of God. *Section 1, Day 26*
libertarians:	Christians who have argued that freedom in Christ means that even unbiblical pleasures can be pursued. *Section 3, Day 21*
mercy of God:	God's withholding of deserved judgment. *Section 3, Day 10/17*
misbelief:	Believing the wrong things. *Section 1, Day 23*
monotheist:	The belief that there is only one God. *Section 1, Day 8; Section 3, Day 8*
omnipotence:	God can do all things which are consistent with His nature. *Section 3, Day 7*
omnipresence:	God is everywhere. He is unlimited and unlimitable in regard to space. *Section 2, Day 7; Section 3, Day 12/25*
omniscience:	God knows all; He is unlimited and unlimitable in regard to knowledge. *Section 3, Day 6/25*
orthodoxy:	A term meaning "right praise." *Section 1, Day 12*
paraphrase:	The rendering of the Bible in one language to a different form in that same language. *Section 2, Day 16*
philosophy:	The love of wisdom. *Section 1, Day 9*
piety:	Godliness. *Section 1, Day 7*

plenary:	Inspiration extends to all parts of the Bible alike. *Section 2, Day 15*
progressive revelation:	God did not tell us all that we needed to know in the Old Testament, but gradually communicated His full truth through all sixty-six books of the entire Bible. *Section 2, Day 20*
providence:	God's continuing care of His creation. *Section 3, Day 28*
rationalism:	A way of looking at life that says we should not believe anything which we cannot explain with our finite minds. *Section 2, Day 3*
reason:	The capacity for rational thought. *Section 2, Day 3*
rite:	A practice of the Christian faith. *Section 1, Day 16*
ritual:	A practice of the Christian faith. *Section 1, Day 16*
self-sufficiency:	God depends on nothing outside Himself for His being. *Section 3, Day 2*
Shema:	The Hebrew declaration of God's oneness: "Hear, O Israel: the LORD our God, the LORD is one" (Deuteronomy 6:4). *Section 3, Day 8*
special revelation:	God's communication of Himself and His mind to some people at particular times and places. *Section 2, Day 14*
stoicism:	A philosophy which emphasizes the power of destiny and denies the immortality of the human soul. *Section 1, Day 9*
superstition:	Any belief, practice or rite unreasonably upheld by faith in magic, chance or dogma. *Section 1, Day 29*
systematic theology:	A discipline which takes the doctrinal material of the Bible and arranges that material into logical categories. *Section 2, Day 7*

theocracy: A government by God. *Section 3, Day 9*

theodicy: A defense of God's goodness in the face of evil's reality. *Section 3, Day 9/20*

theologian: A Christian who seriously studies the truths of God. Every Christian should be a theologian. *Section 1, Day 4*

Theologian: Those Christians who pursue formal education in the Bible and theology and teach courses in doctrine. *Section 1, Day 4*

theology: The study of the truths of God as set forth in the Bible. The term means "the study of God and the things of God." *Section 1, Day 3*

"to plunder the Egyptians": To use whatever resources are available (even from non-Christian thinkers) to assist the teaching of biblical truth. *Section 1, Day 24*

tolerance: Defending the right of others to believe what they want to believe. *Section 1, Day 5*

tradition: The regular practices of the believers when they gather together. *Section 1, Day 19*

transcendence: A term emphasizing God's distance or independence from His creation. *Section 3, Day 2*

translation: Generally synonymous with "version" (the rendering of the Bible from one language to another). *Section 2, Day 16*

Trinity: Although the term "trinity" is not used in the Bible, the concept that God is one and also three is clearly taught. *Section 3, Day 9*

undulation: The alternating spiritual highs and lows of the believer who is seriously following God. *Section 2, Day 27*

unit-reading: To read an entire book of the Bible through at one sitting. *Section 2, Day 19*

unity: Christians should show oneness in the essential doctrines of the Christian faith and charity in the areas about which they are free to hold various opinions (the distinctives). *Section 1, Day 18*

veracity: God represents things as they really are. *Section 3, Day 22*

verbal: The actual language form used was divinely directed. *Section 2, Day 15*

version: Generally synonymous with "translation" (the rendering of the Bible from one language to another). *Section 2, Day 16*

worship: The redeemed heart's response to the person and work of God. *Section 3, Day 26*

wrath of God: God's righteous response to all that contradicts His holiness. *Section 3, Day 18/19*